CRICUT MAKER 3 HANDBOOK

A Dummy's-Manual To Mastering Cricut Maker 3, Cricut Design Space with In-Depth Project and Tips

Shelli Lynne

COPYRIGHT:

All rights reserved (Copyright 2023 © Shelli Lynne). This book is protected by copyright and is for personal use only. No part of this book may be reproduced, distributed, sold, quoted, or paraphrased without the consent of the author or publisher.

LEGAL NOTICE:

At the time of publication, the information in this book is believed to be accurate. However, neither the author nor the publisher can be held liable for any errors or omissions.

DISCLAIMER NOTICE:

This book is a guide for using Cricut Maker 3. Consult a professional Cricut Crafter for proper use of the Design Space software.

The author is not responsible for any reliance on the statements or representations made in this manual. It is recommended that the information provided be used in consultation with a Cricut Professional.

Your Free Bonuses

FREE BONUS

As a gesture of gratitude for your purchase, you will be given the opportunity to receive three incredible bonuses:

BONUS # 1 — Receive a complimentary guide containing detailed instructions on obtaining my personal guide to using Cricut Design Space and other accessories, which I use on a daily basis.

BONUS # 2 — Get access to a vast collection of high-quality SVG files without any cost. Stay motivated with unrestricted usage of over 2000 images, fonts, and expertly designed graphics.

BONUS # 3 - Become part of my amazing mentorship and business class for Free. You'll have access to thousands of project ideas that won't cost you a penny!

SCAN THE QR CODE AND GET YOUR GIFT!

Please use your phone's camera to scan this QR code to access your bonus content.

Contents

INTRODUCTION — 1

CHAPTER ONE — 3
The Cricut Machine
    What Can I Make With Cricut Machine:
    Model Overview:
    How Does Cricut Machine Work?

CHAPTER TWO — 12
Unboxing The Cricut
    What is in the Cricut Box:

CHAPTER THREE — 15
Components of the Cricut Machine

Author's Note — 25

CHAPTER FOUR — 27
Getting Started
    Getting Prepared:
    Initial Setup of Cricut Maker 3:

CHAPTER FIVE — 38
Cricut Blades
- Types of Cricut Blades:
- Fine Point Blade:
- Rotary Blade:
- QuickSwap Tools:
- Knife Blade:
- Foil Transfer Tool:
- Scoring Stylus:

CHAPTER SIX — 53
Changing Cricut Blade
- Why Change Cricut Blade:
- How to Change Point Blade:
- How to Change Knife Point Blade:
- How to Change Rotary Blade:
- Caution Changing Cricut Blades:

CHAPTER SEVEN — 68
Cricut Materials
- Types of Cricut Material:
- Vinyl Material:
- Cardstock Material:
- Iron-On Material (Heat Transfer Vinyl):
- Infusible Ink Sheets:

Fabric Material:

Adhesive Foil:

Leather:

CHAPTER EIGHT — 96
Maintaining Cricut Machine
- General Care for Cricut Machine:
- How to Clean Cricut Blades:
- How to Clean Every Part of Your Cricut Machine:
- How to Clean a Cricut Mat:

Author's Note — 107

CHAPTER NINE — 109
Cicut Design Space: Introduction
- Why Cricut Design Space:
- Install Cricut Design Space For iPad/iPhone:
- Frequently Asked Questions (FAQ):

CHAPTER TEN — 118
Design Space: Canvas Overview
- The Canvas:
- The Left Panel:

CHAPTER ELEVEN — 130
Design Space: Top / Editing Bar
- Placing Text or Images on Design Screen:

How to Perform Linetype from Android/iOS

Working with Fonts in Design Space:

Adding Text to Cricut Design Space:

How to Edit Text in Cricut Design Space:

How to Select Fonts:

CHAPTER TWELVE — 151
Design Space Tips

How to use Color Sync Panel

How to Use Patterns in Cricut Design Space

How to Mirror Designs

Working with Text in Design Space

Design Space Tricks

CHAPTER THIRTEEN — 160
Turning Hobby Into Business With Cricut Maker 3

The Concept of Work:

Can I Turn My Craft into a Profitable Business?

Starting A Cricut Business:

Choosing Your Cricut Clientele:

Tips For Making Money and Setting Cricut Business:

CHAPTER FOURTEEN — 179
Selling Your Craft

Where can I sell my Cricut Craft?

Online Marketplaces:
Social Media Platforms:
Your Own Website or Online Shop:
Craft Fairs and Local Markets:
Consignment Shops and Boutiques:
How Should I Price My Cricut Item?
Should I Quit My Day Job?

CHAPTER FIFTEEN 197
Cricut Project Idea
- Leather Cuff Bracelet:
- Cosmetic Bag:
- Geometric Buffalo Pillows:
- Customized T-Shirt:
- Customized Mugs:
- Customized Mug:
- Halloween Mask:
- Fifty (50) Project Idea:

RATE THIS BOOK 233
About the Author 235

INTRODUCTION

In this comprehensive handbook, we embark on a journey through the extraordinary capabilities of the Cricut Maker 3, a cutting-edge crafting machine that has revolutionized the way artists, hobbyists, and DIY enthusiasts bring their imaginative visions to life.

Whether you're a seasoned crafter or just starting out, this book serves as your ultimate guide to mastering the Cricut Maker 3. From its basic features to advanced techniques, we explore every facet of this incredible machine, empowering you to unlock its full potential.

Within these pages, you'll find step-by-step instructions, practical tips, and inspiring project ideas that will inspire you to push the boundaries of your creativity. Learn how to effortlessly cut a wide range of materials, including paper, vinyl, fabric, leather, and even wood.

Discover how to design and personalize your projects using the intuitive Design Space software, and delve into the vast library of ready-to-make designs and fonts available to you.

Whether you aspire to create stunning home decor, personalized gifts, stylish apparel, or intricate paper crafts, the Cricut Maker 3 is your indispensable companion.

So, let's embark on this exciting journey together and unlock the door to a realm where imagination knows no bounds. Get ready to unleash your creativity and bring your artistic dreams to life with the Cricut Maker 3.

CHAPTER ONE
The Cricut Machine

The Cricut machine is a versatile and innovative crafting tool that has transformed the way people create and personalize various projects. The cricut machines are designed to cut a wide range of materials with precision, allowing users to bring their creative ideas to life.

The Cricut machine uses a blade to cut a variety of materials, including paper, vinyl, fabric, and leather. It can be used for to make various projects, such as card making, scrapbooking, and home decor.

Cricut machines are popular among crafters and hobbyists, as they allow them to create professional-looking projects with ease. They are also used by businesses for marketing and promotional materials.

What Can I Make With Cricut Machine:

From cutting intricate designs out of various materials to adding custom details and embellishments, the Cricut machine can make anything such as;

- **Customized Greeting Cards:** Design and cut out personalized cards for birthdays, holidays, weddings, and more.

- **Home Decor:** Create beautiful wall decals, vinyl lettering, custom artwork, and decorative items to enhance your living space.

- **Scrapbooking and Paper Crafts:** Cut out intricate shapes, borders, and embellishments for scrapbook pages, handmade journals, and other paper crafts.

- **Personalized Apparel:** Design and cut heat-transfer vinyl to customize t-shirts, hoodies, tote bags, and hats with your own unique designs or slogans.

- **Party Decorations:** Make eye-catching banners, cupcake toppers, party favors, and other decorations.

- **Vinyl Decals:** Create custom decals for car windows, laptops, water bottles, and other surfaces.

- **Leather Crafts:** Cut intricate patterns for leather accessories such as wallets, keychains, bracelets, and earrings.

- **Customized Gifts:** Personalize mugs, tumblers, wine glasses, and other gift items with names, quotes, or monograms.

- **Classroom Materials:** Design and cut out educational materials, bulletin board decorations, labels, and teaching aids for teachers and homeschoolers.

- **Vinyl Stencils for DIY Projects:** Cut out stencils for painting on wood, fabric, or other surfaces, allowing you to create unique signs, home decor, and artwork.

These are just a few examples of the endless possibilities that await you with the Cricut machine.

Model Overview:

Cricut machines are available in various models with different features and capabilities. Here are some of the popular models:

(1) Cricut Maker:

The Cricut Maker is the flagship model known for its exceptional cutting power and versatility. It features an adaptive tool system, allowing for precise cutting of an extensive range of materials, including fabric, wood, leather, and more. The Maker also offers additional tools like the rotary blade and knife blade, expanding its capabilities.

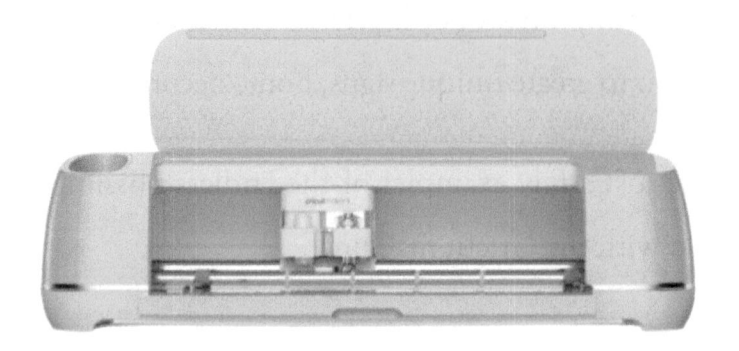

Cricut Maker 3

(2) Cricut Joy:

The Cricut Joy is a compact and portable cutting machine designed for smaller projects. It can cut materials up to 5.5 inches wide and offers a simplified setup and operation, making it perfect for quick and easy crafts.

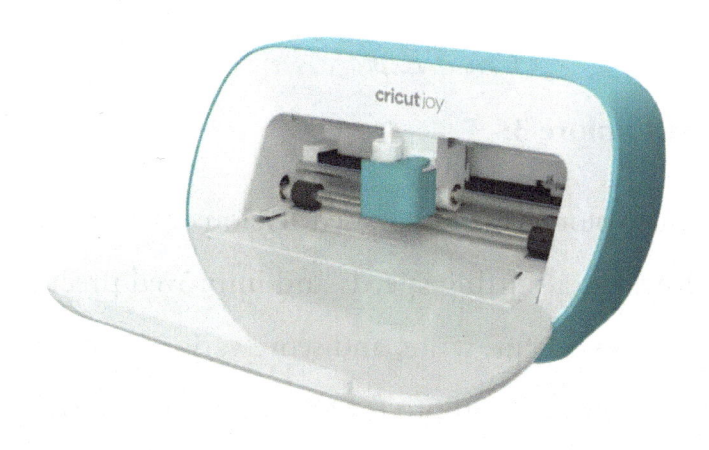

Cricut Joy

(3) Cricut Explore Air 2:

The Cricut Explore Air 2 is a versatile cutting machine that allows for cutting, writing, and scoring a wide range of materials. It offers wireless connectivity, fast cutting speeds, and a wide selection of compatible tools, making it a popular choice among crafters.

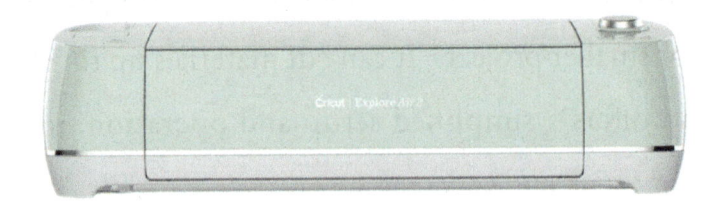

Cricut Explore Air 2

(4) Cricut Explore 3:

The Cricut Explore 3 is an upgraded version of the Explore Air 2, providing faster cutting speeds and improved precision. It offers the ability to cut, write, and score various materials and comes with built-in Bluetooth for wireless connectivity.

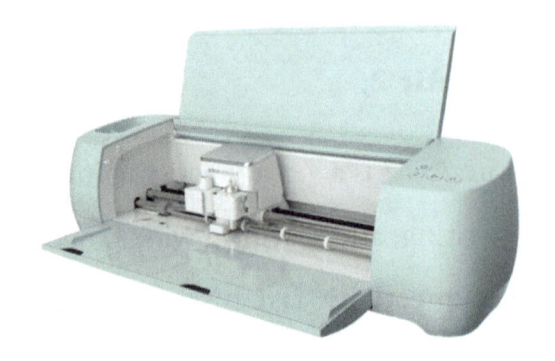

Cricut Explore 3

(5) Cricut Cuttlebug:

The Cricut Cuttlebug is a manual die-cutting and embossing machine. It operates by using cutting dies and embossing folders to create intricate shapes and designs on paper, cardstock, and other materials. It is a popular choice for those who prefer manual operation.

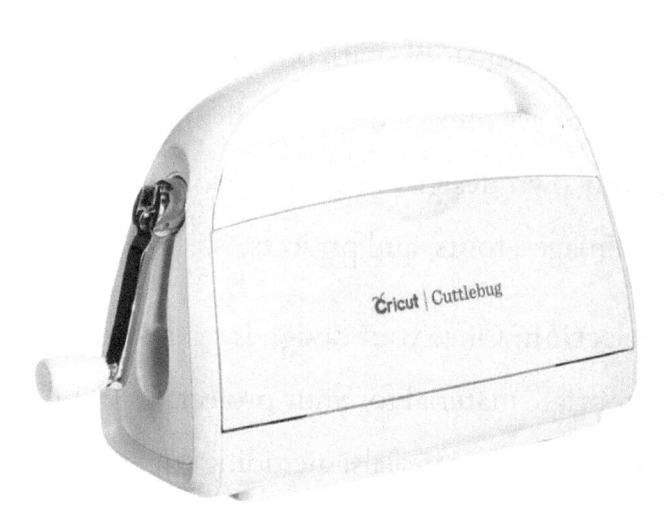

Cricut Cuttleug

Each Cricut machine is designed to cater to different crafting needs and skill levels. Consider your desired projects, materials, and features when selecting the right Cricut machine for you.

How Does Cricut Machine Work?

The Cricut machine operates through a combination of hardware and software to bring your creative projects to life. Here's a general overview of how the Cricut machine works:

Designing: The first step is to create or choose a design for your project. This can be done using the Cricut Design Space software, which is compatible with both computers and mobile devices. Design Space offers a user-friendly interface where you can create your own designs or choose from a vast library of pre-designed images, fonts, and projects.

Material Selection: Once your design is ready, you need to select the appropriate material for your project. Cricut machines can cut a wide range of materials, including paper, vinyl, fabric, cardstock, leather, and more. Make sure to choose a material that is compatible with your machine and matches the requirements of your design.

Loading the Material: After selecting your material, you will need to prepare it for cutting. This involves placing the material onto a cutting mat or using a specific tool, depending on the type of material and project. The cutting mat helps secure the material in place during the cutting process and ensures accurate results.

Cutting: With the material loaded and the design ready, it's time to cut. The Cricut machine uses a precise cutting mechanism controlled by the software to follow the design's instructions. It moves the cutting blade or other tools along the material, cutting out the desired shapes, letters, or patterns with great accuracy. The cricut machines also offer additional capabilities like scoring, drawing, and engraving depending on your project.

Assembly and Finishing: Once the cutting is complete, carefully remove the material from the cutting mat and assemble the pieces according to your design. If necessary, you can apply additional finishing touches like weeding (removing excess material), ironing on heat-transfer vinyl, or gluing the components together.

Throughout the process, the Cricut Design Space software communicates with the Cricut machine, providing instructions on speed, pressure, and tool changes based on the design's specifications. The software and machine work in sync to ensure precise cutting and a seamless crafting experience.

CHAPTER TWO
Unboxing The Cricut

Unboxing a new item comes with huge expectations and curiosity because you want to see what's hidden inside the big box. In this chapter, you will learn the step-by-step guide on how to unbox your Cricut Maker 3.

What is in the Cricut Box:

Here is a step-by-step process on how to unbox the Cricut Maker 3 and the items found inside the box;

Place Cricut Box:

Choose a well-lit and clean area with enough room to accommodate your Cricut Maker 3 and any additional accessories you may have. Place the Cricut box on a flat, clean surface free from clutter to prevent confusion or mix-up with other materials.

Open The Box:

Carefully open the box from the top, pulling it open gradually. Inside the box, you will find an envelope that catches your attention. This envelope holds a few essential items for your Cricut Maker 3 experience.

The Envelop:

This envelope contains valuable content as a starting point for your Cricut journey. You will see a sample 6-inch piece of Smart Vinyl among these items. This sample smart vinyl is for your first cut testing, allowing you to embark immediately on your first cutting adventure.

Inside the envelope, you will find a quick start guide, which provides concise instructions for setting up your machine. Furthermore, the envelope also contains a warranty and safety card regarding warranty coverage and safety guidelines.

Smart Material:

Pull out the cardboard inserted at both edges of the box and keep them aside. Remove the smart materials, which include a sheet of smart vinyl, transfer tape, a sheet of smart iron-on, and a piece of smart paper sticker cardstock.

Unwrap The Cricut Machine:

The next package in the box is the cricut machine. Gradually pull it out and place it on the surface. The Cricut Maker 3 is packaged with a premium Fine-point blade.

Accessories:

Beneath the Machine is a USB Cable and Power Adapter. These accessories are needed to power the Cricut Machine.

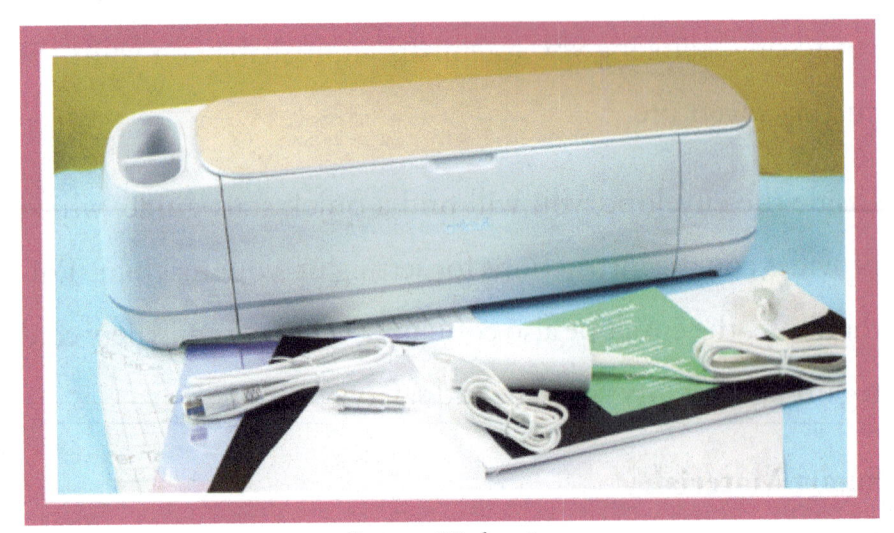

Cricut Unboxing

These are the items that can be found inside the box of the Cricut.

CHAPTER THREE

Components of the Cricut Machine

The Cricut Maker 3 is a powerful crafting machine that comes with various components to enhance its functionality and versatility. In this section, you will be learning about the different components of the Cricut Maker 3.

Learning about the different compartments of the Cricut Maker 3 is a great way to get started. The Cricut Maker 3 has many separate compartments, each serving its purpose. So, let's get started;

The Control Buttons:

The right-hand side of the Machine has four control buttons. These buttons are used to give instructions to the Cricut machine. Here is an explanation of the different control buttons and their purpose:

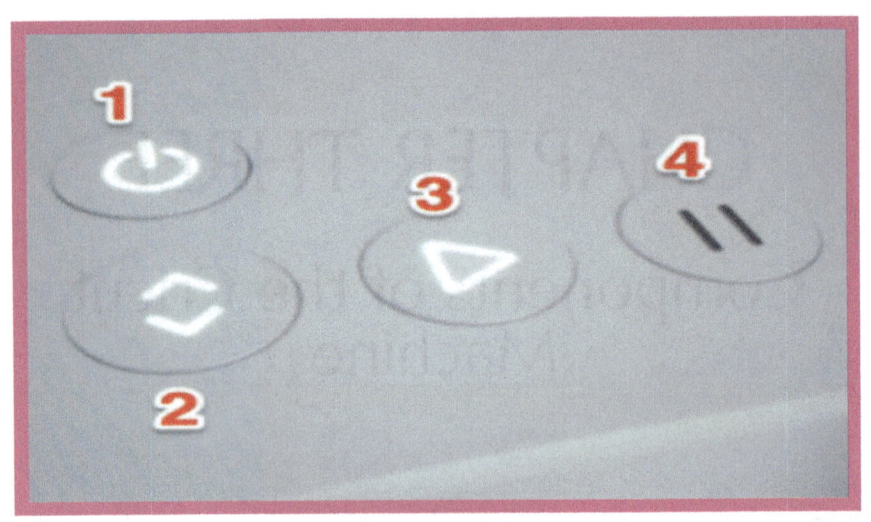

Cricut Control Buttons

1. **Power Button:** The Power Button is used to turn the Cricut Machine on and off. It provides a simple way to control the machine's power supply. This button is important as it allows you to start and shut down the machine safely and conserves energy when not in use.

2. **Load/Unload Button:** This button is used to load cutting material or unload the cutting mat from the machine. When you press this button, the Cricut machine guides the cutting mat into the correct position, ensuring precise and accurate cuts.

3. **Start Button:** This button is used to begin the cutting or writing process. Once you have loaded the material

and selected your design in the Cricut Design Space software, pressing the Start Button initiates the actual cutting or writing operation.

4. **Pause Button:** This button allows you to temporarily pause the cutting or writing process if needed. Pressing this button halts the machine's operation without canceling the entire job.

These control buttons on the right side of the Cricut provide convenience, control, and safety during the crafting process.

Holding Tray:

The Cricut holding tray is an area where materials are placed or inserted into the machine. It is located at the bottom of the device and can hold one roll of vinyl or fabric.

The holding tray features a material guide on both sides of the tray to clamp down the vinyl or fabric during cutting or scoring. When placing material on your Cricut machine, ensure that the material is correctly placed and held by the material guide.

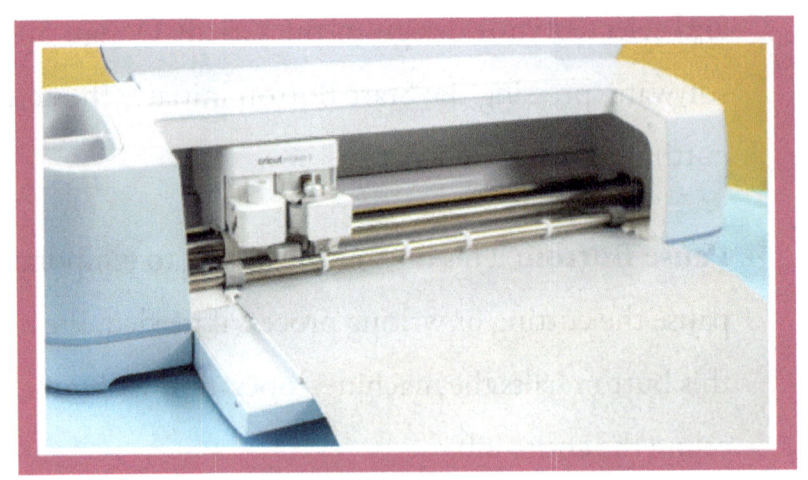

Holding tray

The tray also has a smart tool storage compartment that can be used to store and organize your equipment. There are three compartments in the storage area, and they can be used to store the following:

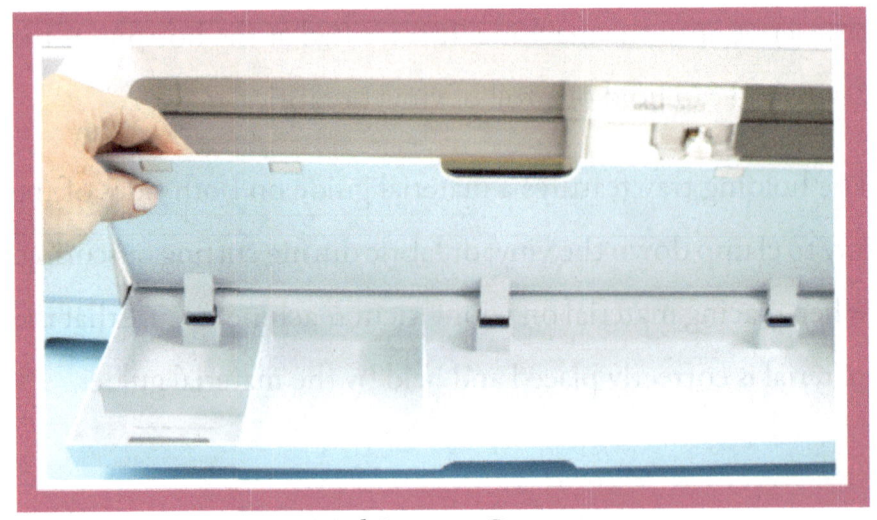

Smart Tool Storage Compartment

- **Compartment 1:** This compartment is the largest, and it can be used to store the Cricut Basic Tool Set, as well as other tools such as the weeding tool, scissors, tweezers, TrueControl Knife, and scoring stylus.

- **Compartment 2:** This compartment is smaller, and it can be used to store the scraper.

- **Compartment 3:** This compartment is the smallest, and it has a magnetic strip that can be used to store the tiny blade replacements.

The smart storage compartment is a great way to keep your tools organized and within reach while you are working on a project. It's important to place the tools in the compartments correctly, especially for the blade housings and Quick Swap housings which will only fit in a specific way.

If you have a lot of tools, it's worth considering a separate storage solution like cases, trays, or inserts. And when you're done using the smart storage compartment, don't forget to close the lid to avoid misplacing any tools.

Deep Storage Compartment:

On the left of the Cricut is a deep storage compartment that is lined with a silicone layer. This compartment is a great place to store larger items, such as pens, markers, and cutting mats. It can hold up to 15 pens and markers, or 2 cutting mats.

Deep Storage Compartment

Tablet Slot:

The tablet slot is located on the top of the machine. This slot is designed to hold a tablet, such as an iPad or Android tablet, so that you can use it to control the Cricut machine and view your projects in real time.

Tablet Slot

Adaptive Tool System:

The adaptive tool system is the driving force of the Cricut machine. There are two major tools in this section;

- **Clamp A:** This segment holds tools like; pens, a scoring stylus, etc. It is important to note that the accessory adapter comes pre-installed in this segment.

- **Clamp B:** This is where the Premium fine-point blade is installed. You can switch out with another tool by pulling the holder and removing the current tools. Put in a new one, and close the holder segment.

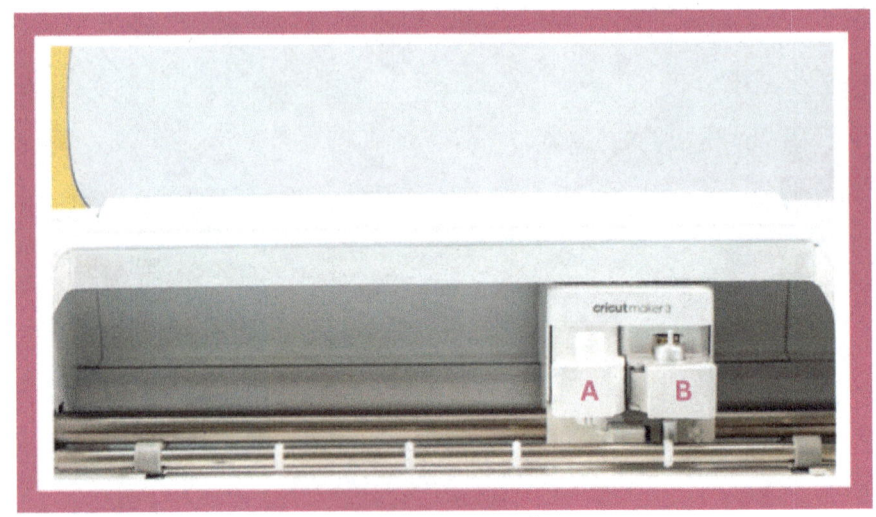

Adaptive Tools

Cricut Sensor:

This Cricut machine has two sensors that assist in aligning the material and ensuring that there is enough material for the cut to be made. The two sensors are as follow:

- **The Print Then Cut sensor:** This sensor is located on the underside of the carriage, and it is used to scan the cut sensor marks on Print Then Cut projects.

- **The Smart Materials sensor:** This sensor is located on the front of the machine, and it is used to detect the presence of Smart Materials.

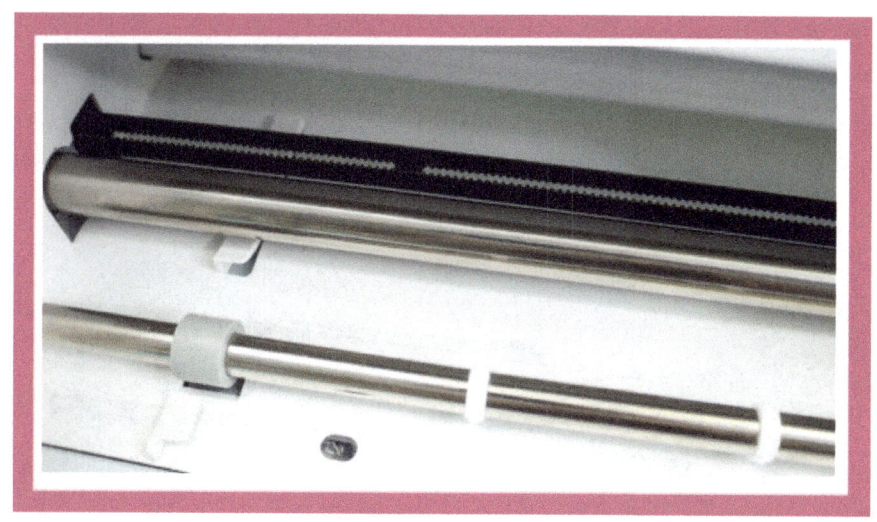

Cricut Sensor

Both of these sensors are essential for the Cricut Maker 3 to function properly. If either sensor is not working, the machine may not be able to cut your projects correctly.

Ports:

The Cricut Machine features a USB port and a power cable on its side. The USB port is used to connect the machine to a computer, which is necessary for certain tasks like cutting designs from a computer file. On the other hand, the power cable is used to provide the Cricut Machine with power.

The Cricut machine also uses Bluetooth connection to connect to a Bluetooth-enabled device such as a laptop or smartphone.

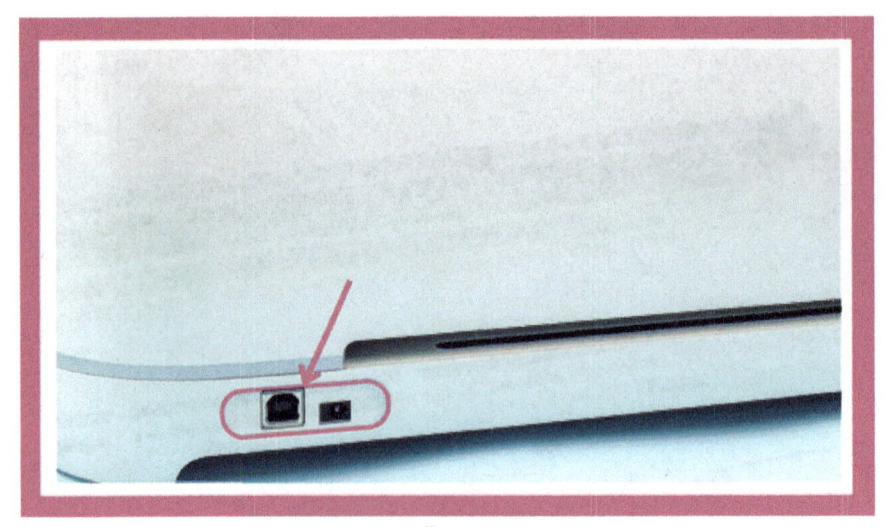

Port

These are the different components of the Cricut Maker 3. If you know where everything is stored, you can find what you need quickly and easily, which can save you time and frustration.

Author's Note

Dear Valued Reader,

Warm greetings to you! I hope this message finds you thriving and full of literary enthusiasm. As a self-publishing author, I write to you today with a humble request for a review of this book.

Behind every book lies a tale of devotion—a testament to the countless hours poured into its creation. My dedicated team and I have spared no effort in meticulously gathering and curating the wealth of information encapsulated within these pages.

Dear valued reader, we aim to provide you with a valuable collection of insightful information, thorough research, and practical knowledge regarding your Cricut Machine. We invested both money and time into creating this book.

Therefore, your feedback holds immeasurable value in our journey. Please take a few moments to leave a review on Amazon. Click on this **Link** or visit (*www.amazon.com/review/create-review?&asin=B0CCMSTXLQ*) to rate this book.

Your comments will tell us how well we perform and guide fellow readers from the extensive wisdom we have painstakingly compiled. We are eagerly awaiting to hear your thoughts and insights. Thank you for considering our request. We appreciate your review and comments, and we will keep them in mind.

CHAPTER FOUR
Getting Started

Setting up your Cricut Maker 3 is an exciting and straightforward process that will have you ready to unleash your imagination in no time. Whether you're a seasoned crafter or just beginning, this chapter is here to ensure a seamless setup experience.

Getting Prepared:

Getting prepared with your Cricut machine is an important step before diving into your crafting projects. By ensuring you have the necessary tools and materials, you'll be ready to unleash your creativity with confidence. Here's a guide to help you get prepared:

Organize Your Workspace:

Create a dedicated workspace for your Cricut Maker 3. Clear the area, ensuring you have enough space for the machine, materials, and any tools you'll be using. Organize your supplies, keeping them within reach for easy access during your crafting sessions.

Organize Workspace

Begin by clearing the workspace of any unnecessary items or clutter. Remove objects that may hinder your movement or access to materials and tools. Create a clean and open area dedicated to your Cricut. Good lighting is crucial for accurate cutting and crafting. Make sure your workspace is well-lit to help you see details clearly. Position your workspace near a window or add additional lighting, such as a desk lamp, to brighten the area.

Connect Your Cricut:

Now, it's time to connect your Cricut Maker 3 to power. Plug one end of the power cord into the back of the machine and the other end into a power outlet. You are now ready to turn on your Cricut Maker 3 by pressing the power button.

Connect Cricut

Create or Gather Design Ideas:

Before you start crafting, brainstorm and gather design ideas for your projects. Whether it's personalized gifts, home decor, or party decorations, having a clear vision will guide your creative process.

Acquire Materials:

Ensure you have the appropriate materials for your projects. The Cricut Maker 3 can cut a wide range of materials, such as paper, vinyl, fabric, cardstock, and more. Stock up on materials that align with your design ideas to bring them to life. In subsequent chapters, you will learn extensively on the different materials for projects

Gather Additional Tools and Accessories:

Depending on your projects, consider any additional tools or accessories that may enhance your crafting experience. These may include different blades, pens for writing or drawing, scoring stylus, weeding tools, and more. Having these on hand will allow you to explore a wide range of techniques and effects.

Install Design Space Software:

If you haven't already, download and install the Cricut Design Space software on your computer or mobile device. This software is essential for creating, customizing, and sending designs to your Cricut Maker 3. In subsequent chapters, you will learn to install design space software and set up a design space account.

Initial Setup of Cricut Maker 3:

Setting up your Cricut Maker 3 Machine is very easy. These simple steps will guide you in setting up your Maker 3 Machine.

Power ON:

Plug the power cable at the back of the Cricut machine and connect it to a power outlet. The next step is to press the "**Power Button**" to turn power on the Cricut machine.

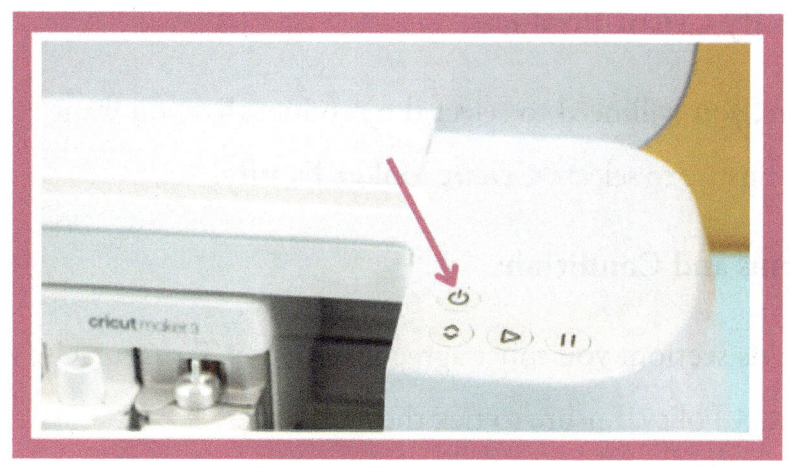

Press the Power Button

Visit the Official Website of Cricut:

To begin setting up your Cricut, visit the official website (https ://design.cricut.com/#/setup). Once there, choose the product you want to set up and select "**Cricut Machine.**"

Visit Cricut Webpage

Specify Cricut Product:

Here, you will need to select the product that you want to set up. Ensure to select **"Cricut Maker Family."**

Terms and Condition:

In this section, you must agree to Cricut's Terms of Use and Privacy Policy. Ensure to tick the small box.

Download Design Space:

After you have accepted the terms, you can select the "Download" button to install the Cricut app.

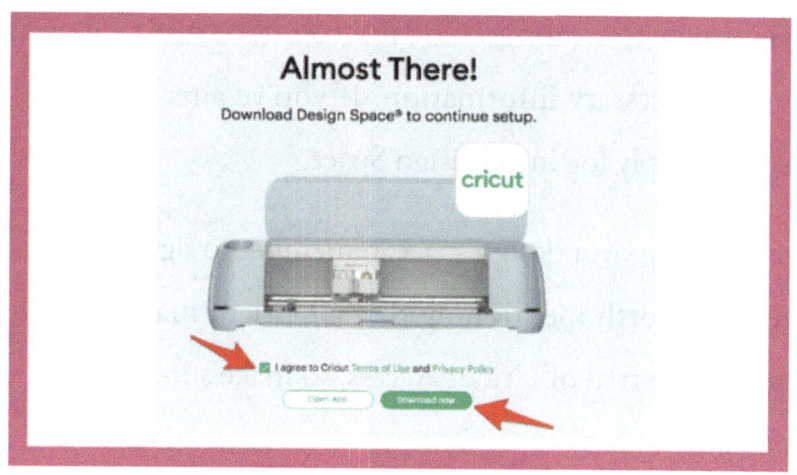

Download Cricut App

Open App:

After downloading and Installing the Cricut app, you will need to open it. In the opening window, you will be prompted to login or create a Cricut ID.

Create Cricut ID

If you're new to creating a Cricut account, be sure to accurately input all necessary information. If you've already created an account, simply log into Design Space.

After creating your design space, remember to sign in to Design Space. It's worth mentioning that all Cricut machines offer a 1-month free trial of Cricut Access, so make sure to utilize this opportunity.

Product Setup:

A new window will open, asking you the type of setup you want. Ensure to Select **"New product Setup."** You will be prompted to choose the Cricut machine to set up; select **"Smart cutting machine"** and click on **"Maker 3"** from the drop-down.

An on-screen window will guide you on how to set up your workspace and connect your Cricut to your Computer. To connect your Cricut to your computer, there are two methods; **Bluetooth** and **USB connection**.

USB Connection:

If you are using a USB connection, ensure to grab the USB Cable and connect one end to your Laptop and the other end to the Cricut machine. After connecting your computer and Cricut, ensure to select your method of connection on the Cricut app, and select "**Connect**."

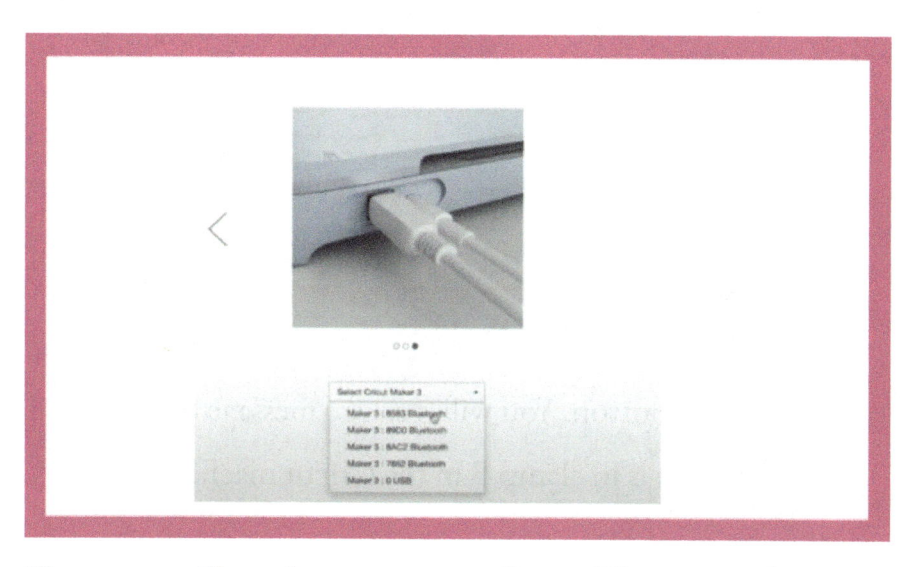

Here, you will need to enter your Cricut ID again and agree to the terms of use of Cricut. Click on the "**Continue button**" to Update and Register your Cricut to your Design space account.

After rebooting, your Design Space app will display a successful connection. Ensure to click on the "**Next**" button. Next, you will be prompted to "**Start your Free Trial**." You can skip this process by selecting **"No Thanks."**

Test Cut:

In this section, you will be prompted to perform a **"Test Cut."**

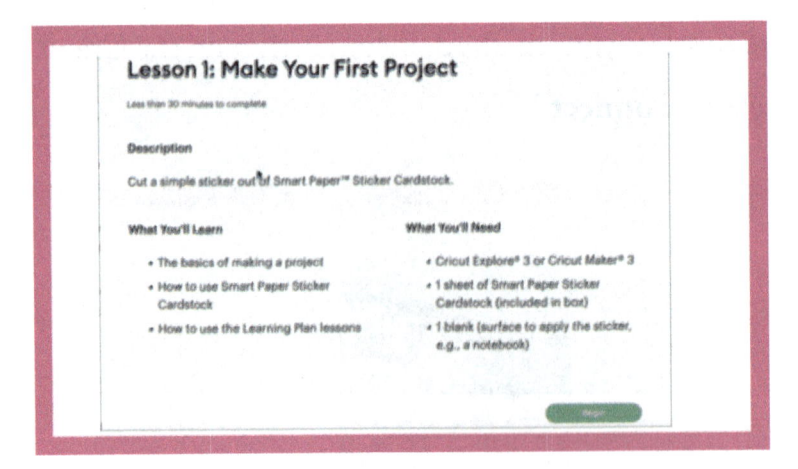

- Pick the Image you would want to cut, and select the **"Next"** button. You will receive a message to confirm if the blade is in clamp B in the Cricut machine.

- After confirmation, you can click on the **"Next"** button. You will be directed to **"Insert your Smart Vinyl Under the Guide."**

- Then, click the **"Load button"** to feed the mat into the Cricut machine. Your Maker 3 will widen the materials and measure them to ensure enough space for cutting.

- Afterward, you can select the "**Start button**" to begin the cutting. When the cutting ends, click the "**Unload button**" to end the operation.

- After unloading the smart vinyl, proceed to weed out the designs.

Congratulations, your Cricut maker 3 is completely set. If you need an assistant at any point, you can contact Cricut customer care immediately and then continue afterward when you have properly received some guidelines.

CHAPTER FIVE
Cricut Blades

The Cricut blades have its unique features and capabilities, allowing you to achieve precise and professional cuts on a wide variety of materials. In this chapter, you will explore the incredible range of blades available for your Cricut machine, and unlocking endless creative possibilities.

Types of Cricut Blades:

The Cricut Machine is compatible with various blades that cater to different cutting needs and materials. Here are the types of blades available:

- Fine Point Blade

- QuickSwap Tools

- Knife Blade and Rotary Blade

These different blades and tools provide the Cricut Maker 3 with exceptional versatility, allowing you to cut, score, engrave, and create intricate designs on various materials. In the next section, you will learn how to choose the right blade for your specific project to achieve precise and professional-quality results.

Fine Point Blade:

The Fine-Point Blade is the standard blade that comes with the Cricut machine. This blade is designed to create the most detailed cuts possible in a wide range of thin to medium-weight fabrics.

The Fine Point Blades are color-coded for easy identification of which blade to use for specific materials. The Cricut Fine Point Blade comes in two color codes: silver and gold.

Silver Fine Point Blade: The silver Fine Point Blade is the standard blade that comes with most Cricut machines, including the Cricut Maker 3. It's suitable for cutting materials such as paper, cardstock, vinyl, and lightweight fabrics.

Gold Fine Point Blade: The gold Fine Point Blade is functionally the same as the silver one and is used for the same cutting applications. However, it is only available in special editions or sets.

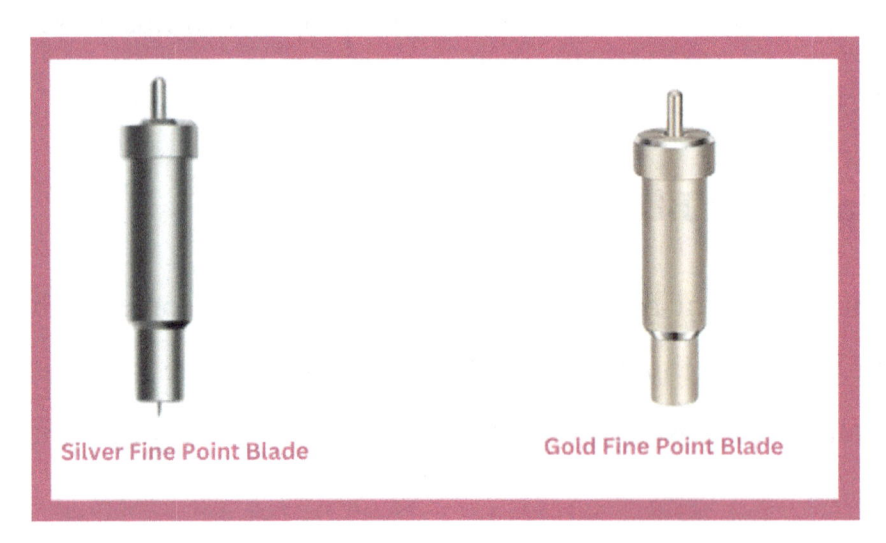

Silver Fine Point Blade

Gold Fine Point Blade

NOTE: Please note that the fine point blades come in different colors but can perform the same function. It is recommended to get both types of blades and assign each one to a specific material. For instance, you can use the Gold Fine Point blade for cutting paper and the Silver Point blade for cardstock and vinyl materials.

Different sets of fine point blades are designed to create the most detailed cuts possible in a wide range of thin to medium-weight fabrics. They are as follows;

Premium Fine Point Blade:

The Premium Fine Point Blade is an upgraded version of the standard Fine Point Blade, offering enhanced durability and longevity. It features a sharper and longer-lasting cutting edge, allowing for cleaner and more precise cuts.

The Premium Fine Point Blade can be used for a wide range of materials, including paper, cardstock, vinyl, iron-on, and lightweight fabrics. It is a versatile blade suitable for most crafting projects, providing excellent results with consistent cutting performance.

Deep Point Blade:

The Deep Point Blade is specifically designed for cutting thicker and denser materials. It has a steeper blade angle, allowing it to penetrate deeper into materials, making it ideal for intricate cuts on materials that require extra depth.

The Deep Point Blade can handle materials such as thicker cardstock, magnet sheets, poster board, chipboard, leather, and craft foam. When working with materials beyond the regular thickness range of the Fine Point Blade, the Deep Point Blade provides better results with cleaner and more precise cuts.

Bonded-Fabric Blade:

The Bonded-Fabric Blade is optimized for cutting fabric materials, particularly those that are bonded or have an iron-on backing. It has a special pink color code, distinguishing it from the standard Fine Point Blade.

The Bonded-Fabric Blade has a unique design with a smaller tip and special blade geometry that helps prevent fabric edges from fraying during cutting. It is perfect for cutting fabrics like cotton, felt, denim, fleece, and other bonded fabrics commonly used in sewing and quilting projects.

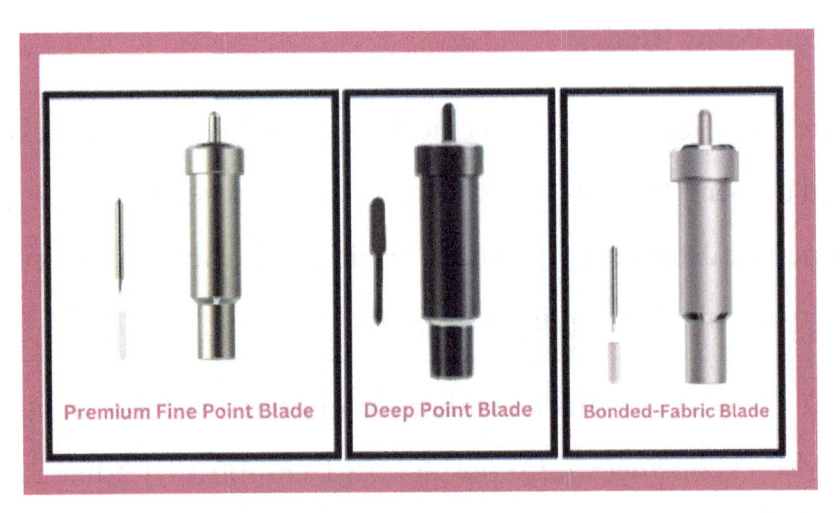

| Premium Fine Point Blade | Deep Point Blade | Bonded-Fabric Blade |

By using these specialized blades within the Fine Point Blade family, you can expand the range of materials you can cut with your Cricut Maker 3.

Rotary Blade:

The Rotary Blade is a specialized cutting tool designed for the Cricut Maker 3 that offers precise and effortless cutting of various types of fabrics. Its versatile blade allows for intricate and delicate cuts without the need for backing material, making it an invaluable tool for sewing, quilting, and other fabric-based projects.

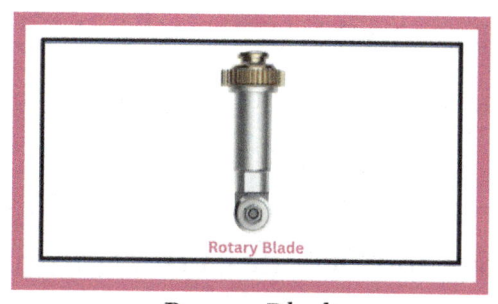

Rotary Blade

Here are some key features and information about the Rotary Blade:

- **Design and Function:** The Rotary Blade features a small, rounded blade housed in a protective housing. Unlike traditional straight blades, the Rotary Blade moves in a rolling motion, similar to a miniature rotary cutter, to achieve smooth and precise cuts on fabrics.

- **Fabric Compatibility:** The Rotary Blade is specifically designed to cut a wide range of fabrics, including cotton, fleece, denim, silk, satin, jersey, and more. It can handle both woven and knit fabrics, allowing for versatile cutting possibilities.

- **Backing Material Not Required:** One of the main advantages of the Rotary Blade is that it can cut fabric without the need for a stabilizing backing material. This eliminates the extra step of applying and removing backing materials, streamlining the cutting process and saving you time.

- **Intricate and Delicate Cuts:** The Rotary Blade excels at cutting intricate and delicate designs on fabrics with exceptional precision. It can create intricate patterns, detailed appliques, and even handle small and intricate shapes with ease.

- **Blade Maintenance:** It is important to keep the Rotary Blade clean and free of fabric debris to ensure optimal cutting performance. Regularly inspect and clean the blade and its housing.

QuickSwap Tools:

The QuickSwap Tools are specially designed for the Cricut Maker 3 machine and allow for easy interchangeability between different blades or tips. You don't need to change the whole housing to switch between them.

This system provides convenience and versatility, allowing you to explore a range of crafting techniques and expand the capabilities of your Cricut Maker 3.

These tools work with the QuickSwap housing, a secure holder that accommodates different blades and tips. Simply insert the desired QuickSwap Tool into the QuickSwap housing to effortlessly change between cutting, scoring, debossing, engraving, and other functions.

With the QuickSwap system, you can expand the capabilities of your Cricut Maker 3 by adding unique effects, decorations, and embellishments to your crafts. Here's an explanation of the QuickSwap Tools available for the Cricut Maker 3, along with their recommended uses and compatible materials:

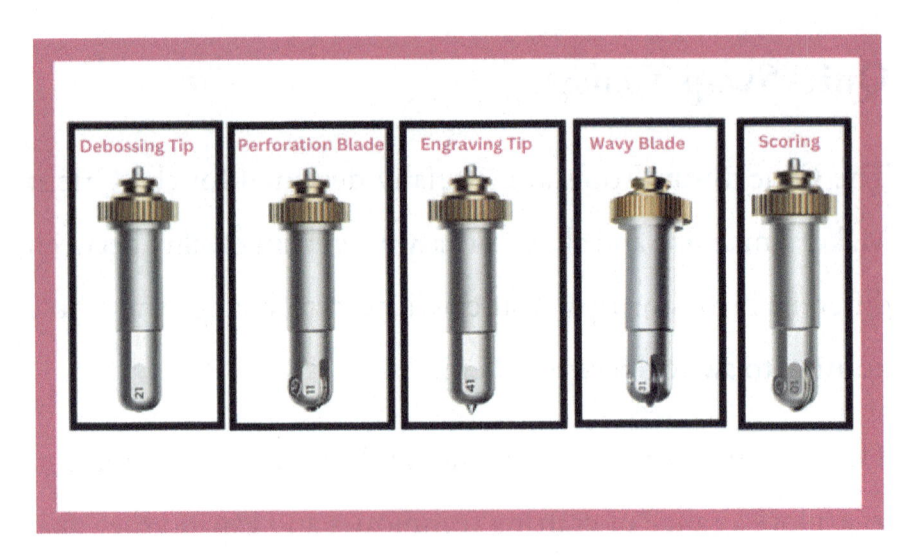

Debossing Tip:

The Debossing Tip creates depressions or indentations on various materials, adding textured designs and patterns to your projects. It is suitable for materials such as cardstock, foil cardstock, coated paper, and specialty papers. Use the Debossing Tip to create decorative elements, embossed sentiments, or intricate patterns that add a unique touch to your creations.

Perforation Blade:

The Perforation Blade allows you to create tear-off edges or perforated lines on materials like paper, cardstock, and lightweight materials. It is perfect for making tear-out elements such as coupons, tickets, raffle cards, and easy-to-remove sections in interactive projects. The Perforation Blade provides clean and precise perforations, making it easy for recipients to tear away designated areas.

Engraving Tip:

The Engraving Tip is designed to engrave intricate designs and patterns onto various materials, including metal, acrylic, leather, aluminum foil, and more. It can add personalized monograms, decorative elements, or detailed artwork to your projects. Experiment with different materials to achieve unique and professional-looking engraved designs.

Wavy Blade:

The Wavy Blade creates a decorative wavy edge on materials such as cardstock, paper, poster board, vinyl, and more. It adds a playful and eye-catching effect to your projects, making it ideal for creating decorative borders, unique party decor, greeting cards, or scrapbook pages. The Wavy Blade adds an extra touch of creativity and texture to your designs.

Scoring and Double Scoring Wheel:

The Scoring Wheel and Double Scoring Wheel create precise score lines on materials such as cardstock, paper, coated paper, and other materials used for folding. The Scoring Wheel provides single-score lines, while the Double Scoring Wheel creates two parallel score lines for clean and precise folding. These tools are essential for creating boxes, cards, envelopes, and other projects that require accurate and crisp fold lines.

These tools provide versatility and add unique elements to your projects, making them stand out.

Knife Blade:

With unmatched simplicity and safety, the extra-deep Knife Blade cuts through solid materials up to 2.5 mm (3/32") thick. It's best for medium-detail cuts in thicker materials including balsa wood, matboard, and chipboard. The maximum cut depth varies according to the material. The knife blade is housed in a silver housing with a gold gear at the top.

Knife Blade

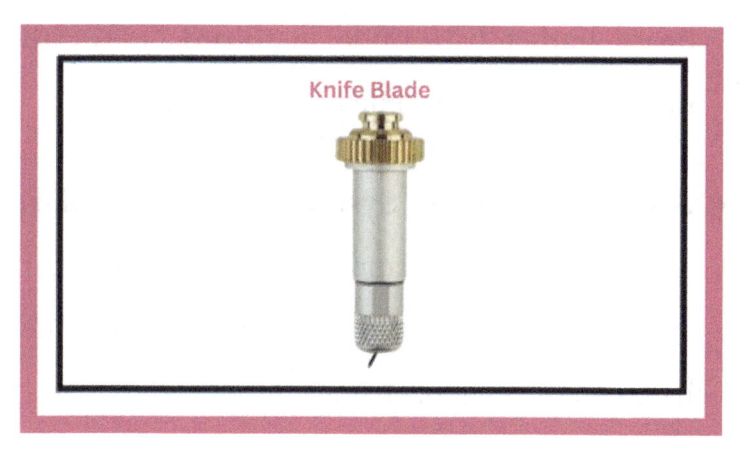

The Knife Blade is a heavy-duty blade that extends the cutting capabilities of the Cricut Maker 3, enabling you to tackle projects involving materials such as chipboard, leather, balsa wood, matboard, and more. Here are some key features and information about the Knife Blade:

- **Design and Function:** The Knife Blade has a sturdy and durable construction with a sharp, pointed tip. It is designed to penetrate thicker materials and make deep, intricate cuts with precision. The blade is housed in a protective housing to ensure safe and controlled cutting.

- **Material Compatibility:** The Knife Blade is specifically designed for cutting thicker and denser materials. It can handle a variety of materials, including chipboard, leather, balsa wood, matboard, heavy cardstock, magnet sheets, and some types of acrylic.

- **Adaptive Pressure System:** The Cricut Maker 3 is equipped with an adaptive pressure system that automatically adjusts the cutting pressure of the Knife Blade based on the material being cut.

- **Multiple Passes:** Cutting thicker and denser materials may require multiple passes with the Knife Blade. The Cricut Design Space software guides you through the process, indicating the number of passes needed for the specific material and project.

- **Protective Measures:** Due to the nature of cutting thicker materials, the Knife Blade may generate more debris compared to other blades.

The Knife Blade expands the capabilities of the Cricut Maker 3, allowing you to create more intricate and robust projects. It enables you to work with a wider range of materials, bringing your ideas to life with exceptional detail and precision.

Foil Transfer Tool:

The Foil Transfer Tool is used in combination with Foil Transfer Sheets to provide a foil effect to projects on various materials. It comes with three replaceable tips: fine, medium, and bold, which are all appropriate for works ranging from basic outlines to complicated patterns. This tool is also compatible with Cricut Explore machines.

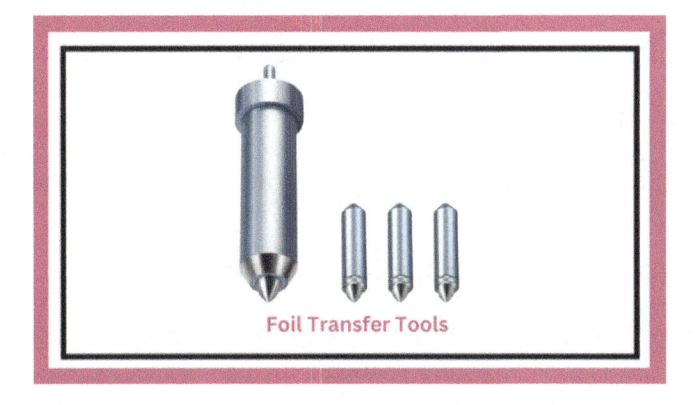

Scoring Stylus:

The Scoring Stylus makes creases and fold lines in a variety of materials, including paper, cardstock, and poster board. This well-known tool is ideal for crafting cards, envelopes, boxes, and other 3D paper crafts.

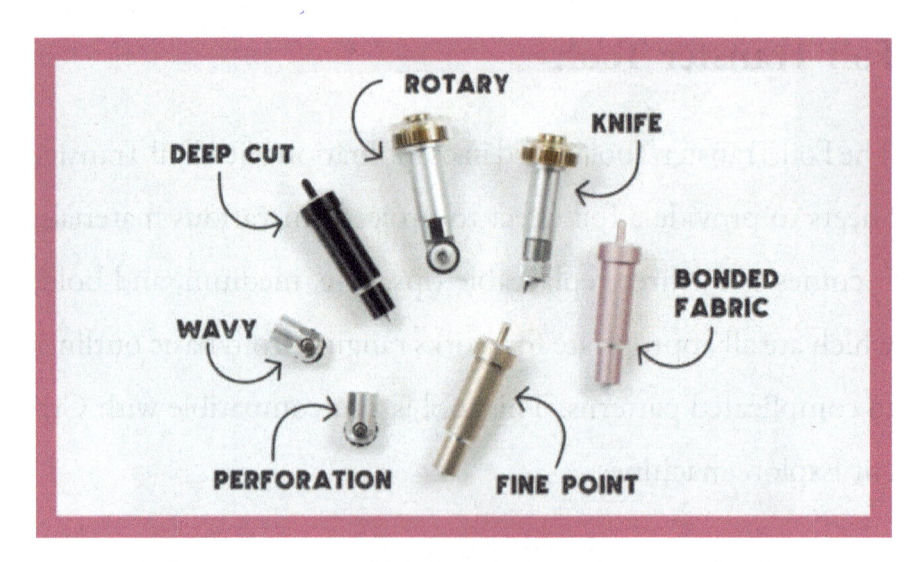

These different types of blades and tools provide the Cricut Maker 3 with exceptional versatility, allowing you to cut, score, engrave, and create intricate designs on various materials.

By choosing the right blade for your specific project, you can achieve precise and professional-quality results, making your crafting experience even more enjoyable and rewarding.

CHAPTER SIX
Changing Cricut Blade

Changing the Cricut blade is a simple but important task that ensures optimal cutting performance for your projects. In this chapter, you learn how to change the blade of Cricut Machine.

Why Change Cricut Blade:

There are several reasons why you may need to change your Cricut blade:

1. **Dullness:** Over time, with repeated use, the blade may become dull and lose its cutting effectiveness. Dull blades can result in incomplete or uneven cuts, affecting the quality of your projects. Changing to a new, sharp blade ensures clean and precise cuts.

2. **Wear and Tear:** The blade may experience wear and tear due to the materials being cut. This can lead to blade damage or bending, affecting its cutting performance. Replacing the blade helps maintain optimal cutting quality.

3. **Different Materials:** Different materials have varying cutting requirements. Blades designed for specific materials, such as the Deep Point Blade for thicker materials or the Bonded-Fabric Blade for fabrics, can provide better results. Switching to a specialized blade ensures accurate and efficient cutting for specific material types.

4. **Project Variety:** As you explore different projects and materials, you may require different blade types to achieve desired results. Having a range of blades allows you to experiment with various materials, thicknesses, and techniques, expanding your creative possibilities.

Regularly changing the blade when needed ensures optimal cutting performance, allowing you to consistently create high-quality crafts with your Cricut machine.

How to Change Point Blade:

To change the blade in your Cricut machine, follow these steps:

- **Power Off and Unplug:** Ensure that your Cricut Maker 3 is powered off and unplugged from the power source for safety.

- **Locate the Blade Housing:** The blade housing is the compartment where the blade is inserted. It is located on the carriage of the Cricut Maker 3.

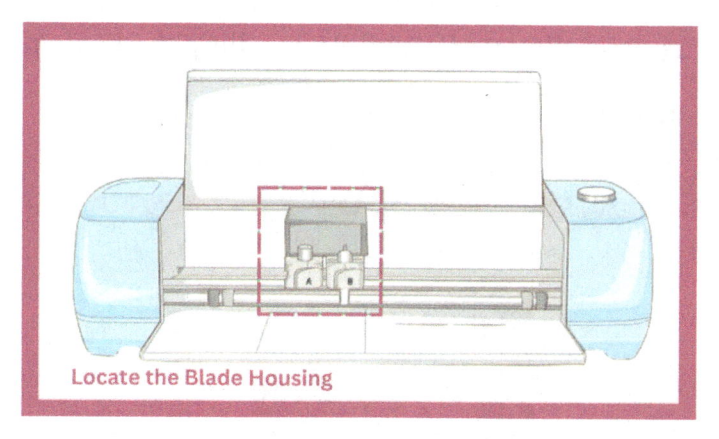

Locate the Blade Housing

- **Open the Clamp:** On the top of the blade housing, you will find a clamp or lever that secures the blade in place. Gently lift or push the clamp to open it. This will release the current blade.

Open the Clamp

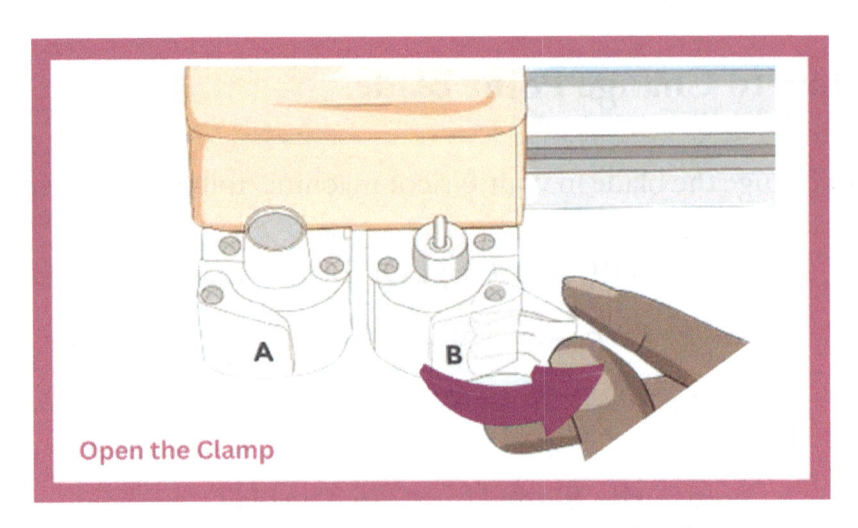

- **Remove the Blade Housing:** Once the clamp is open, carefully remove the blade housing. You can gently pull it out with your fingers or tweezers for better grip and control. Be cautious while handling the blade to avoid any injuries.

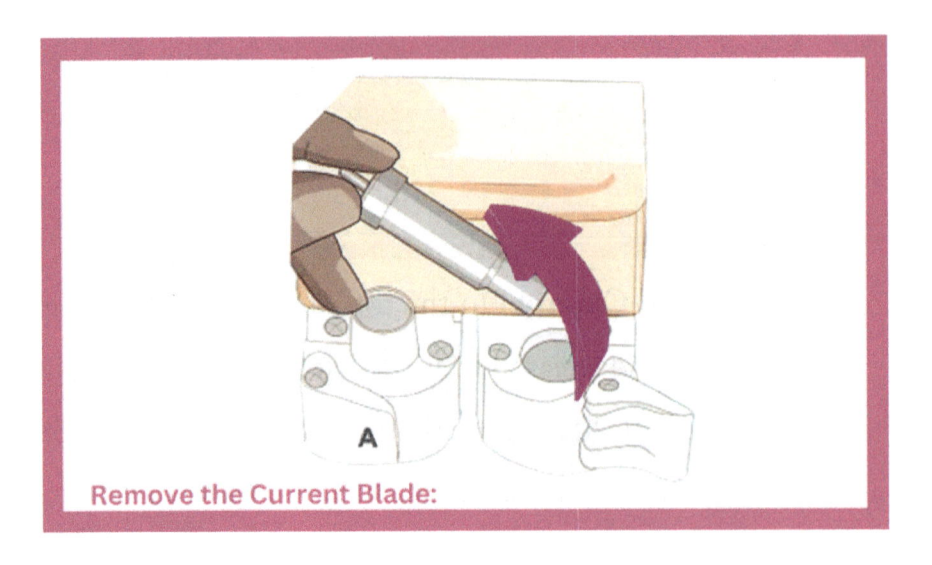

Remove the Current Blade:

- **Remove Existing Blade:** To release the current blade, push down on the plunger at the top of the housing. You will see a small metal piece sticking out on the lower side of the blade housing. Ensure to use pressure on the plunger to help release the blade. It should come out easily, but if it doesn't, carefully hold the blade and remove it from the housing with your other fingers.

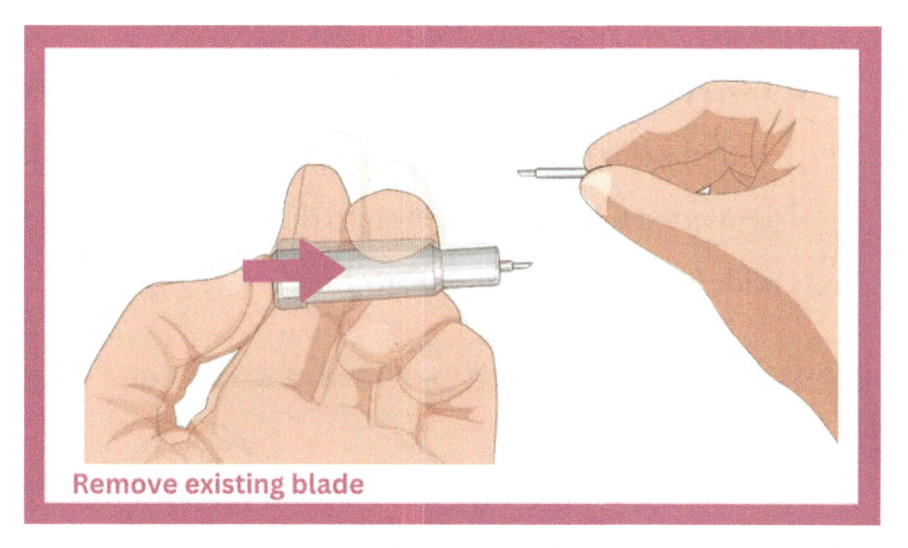

Remove existing blade

- **Unpack New Blade:** Be careful when handling the new blade while removing it from its packaging. Once it is out of the package, you will notice a protective cover on the cutting end that requires removal. Hold the blade delicately, focusing on the cutting end, as you prepare it for installation.

Unpack New Blade

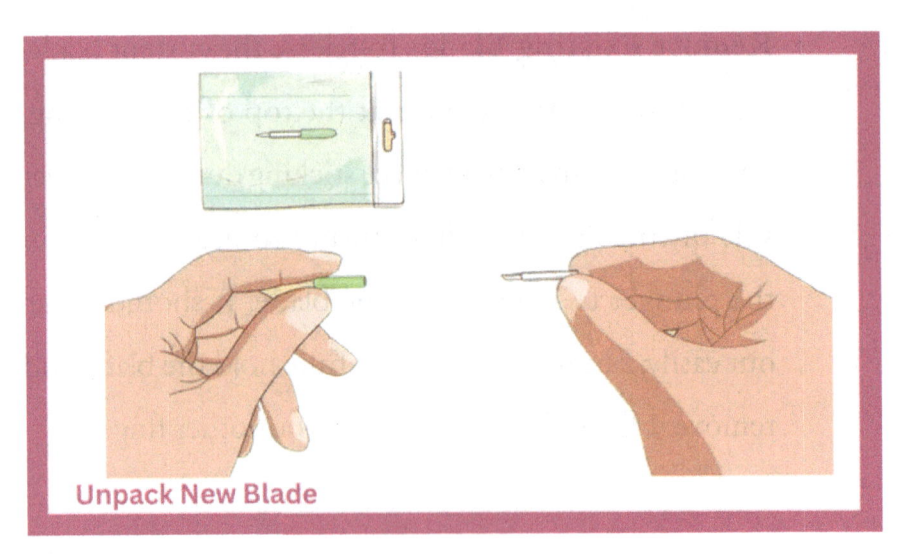

- **Insert the New Blade:** Take the new blade and align it with the slot in the blade housing. Make sure the blade is inserted fully and securely into the housing. It should slide in smoothly without any force.

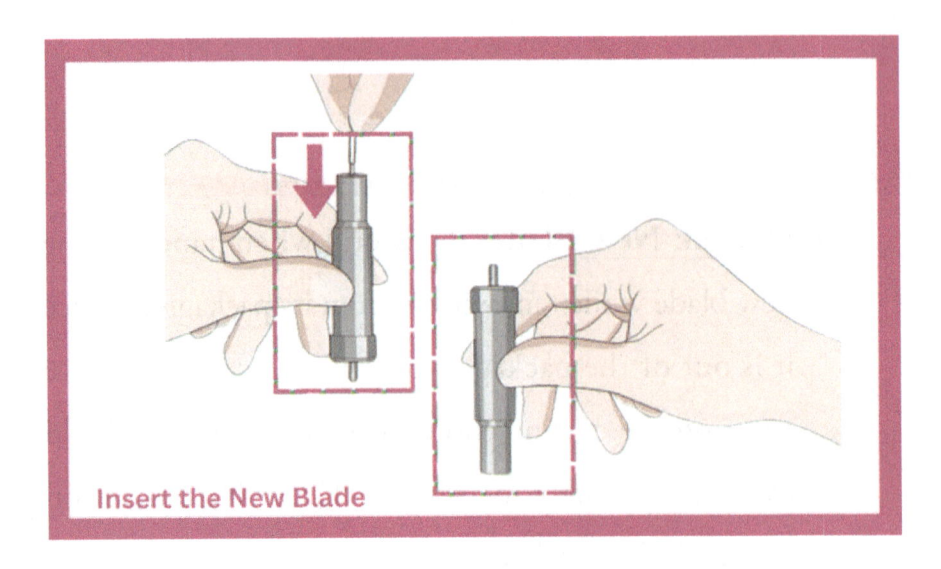

Insert the New Blade

- **Close the Clamp:** Once the new blade is inserted, lower the clamp or lever on the housing blade to secure it. Ensure that the clamp is fully closed and the blade is securely locked.

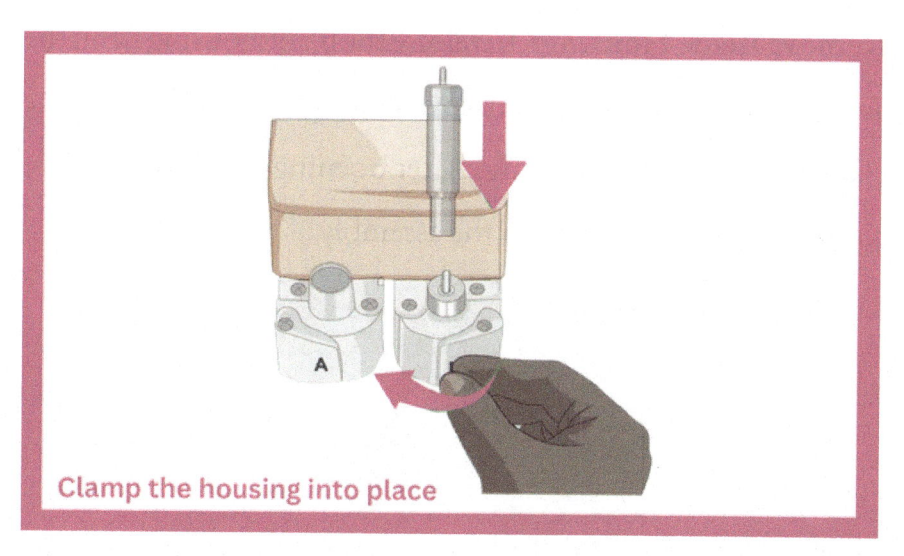

Clamp the housing into place

After changing the blade, it is recommended to perform a test cut on a scrap piece of material to ensure that the blade is properly installed and cut accurately. This will help you verify that everything is working as expected before proceeding with your actual project.

How to Change Knife Point Blade:

To change the knife point blade in your Cricut machine, follow these steps:

Remove Blade Housing: To release the blade housing from the assembly, pull the clamp B tab towards you. This will release the clamp that holds the housing. After opening the clamp, ensure to remove the housing from the assembly.

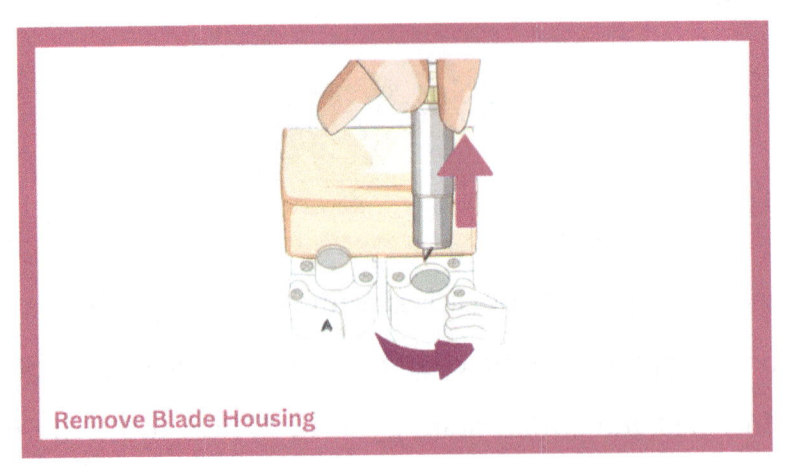

Remove Blade Housing

Insert Protective Cover onto the Blade: When replacing knife-point blades, take extra care due to their larger cutting surface. After removing the blade housing from the cutting assembly, carefully place a provided protective cap over the cutting blade. The replacement blade package will include the appropriate protective cap.

Insert Protective Cover onto the Blade

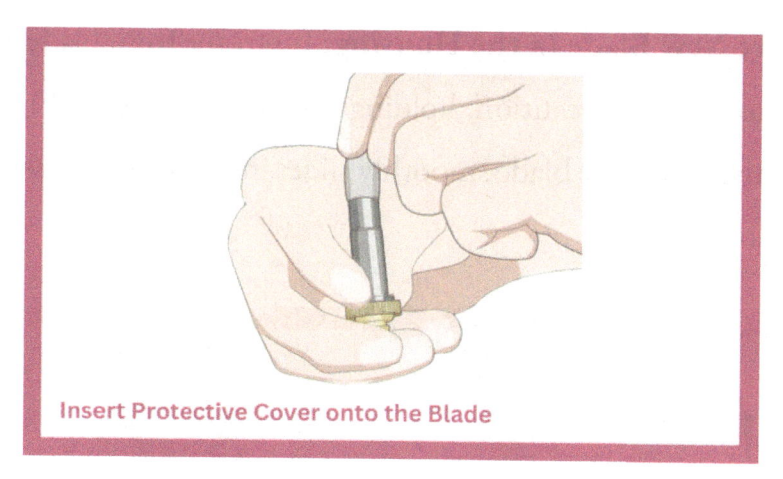

Detach the Previous Blade: You can detach the former blade by twisting the protective cap that covers it counterclockwise. The cap securely holds the screw, allowing the blade to be released. After unscrewing, the old blade will easily come out of the housing and can be discarded or kept for future use. Remember to keep the locking screw inside the protective cap to secure the new blade in place.

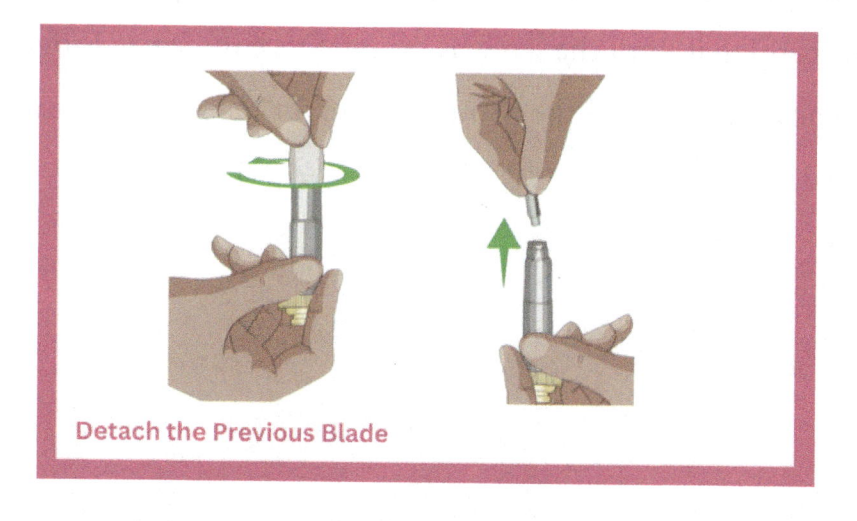

Detach the Previous Blade

Insert New Blade in the Housing: Insert the fresh blade into the housing with caution, holding it by the sharp end. Ensure that the rib on the blade smoothly slides into the groove within the housing.

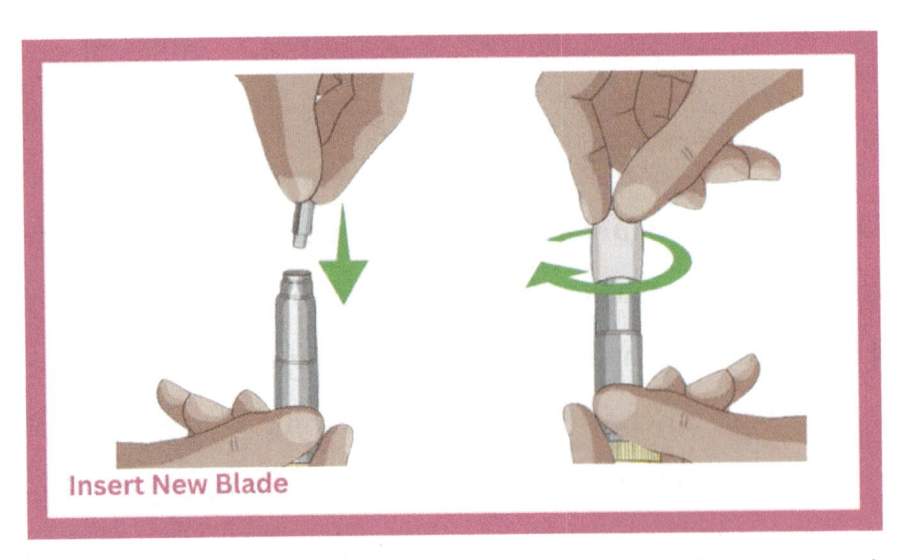

Insert New Blade

Next, slide the protective cap back onto the end, aligning it with the screw. Once the screw is properly positioned, tighten the cap by turning it until the screw is secure. Once the screw is tight, remove and discard the protective cap, or retain it for future blade changes.

How to Change Rotary Blade:

To change the Rotary blade in your Cricut machine, follow these steps:

Take the Blade Housing: Remove the blade housing from the cutting assembly, a labeled box located at the front of the machine. Gently pull the tab marked "B" to release the clamp on the housing assembly. Lift the blade housing out of the assembly, ensuring to keep your fingers and body parts clear of the cutting blade at the bottom.

Take the blade housing out

Cover the Blade with a Protective Cap: To ensure safety during the blade change, it is important to keep the sharp and rotating rotary blade covered. Remove the cap from the new blade and cautiously position it over the existing blade attached to the machine.

Put a protective cover over the blade

Detach the Old Blade: You can detach the old blade by unscrewing it from the blade assembly using the provided screwdriver. As the screw loosens, the old blade will fall into the protective cover. Remember to keep track of the screw for attaching the new blade. Remove the protective cap, discard or store it along with the old blade.

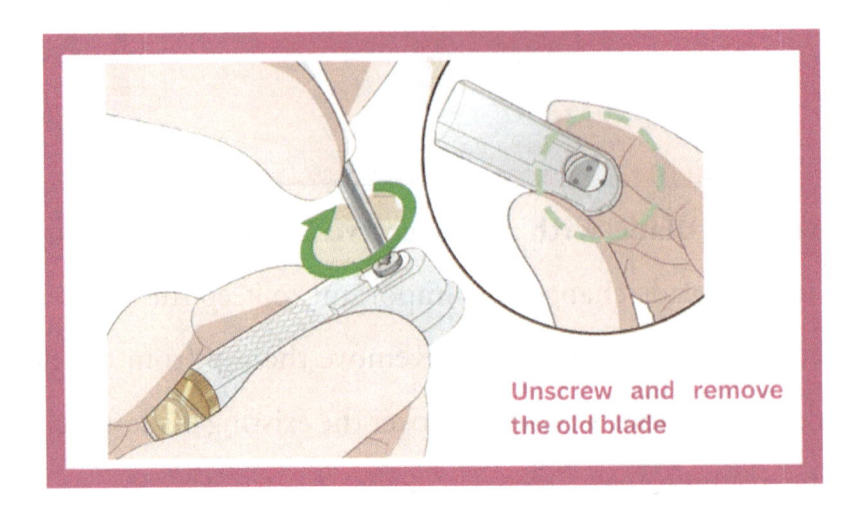

Unscrew and remove the old blade

Attach New Blade: Install the new blade by sliding it onto the blade housing while keeping it within the protective cap. Secure it tightly in place using the screw that was previously removed from the old blade.

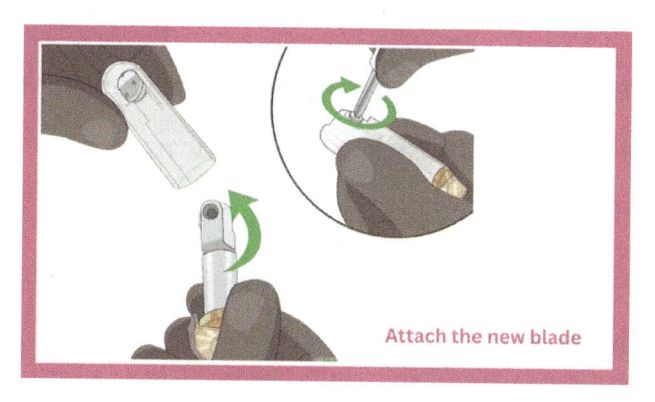

Attach the new blade

Put the blade into the machine: Reinsert the blade assembly into the machine. After installing the new blade, carefully remove the protective cap without touching the blade. Then, insert the blade housing back into the cutting assembly and securely close clamp "B" to ensure it stays in place.

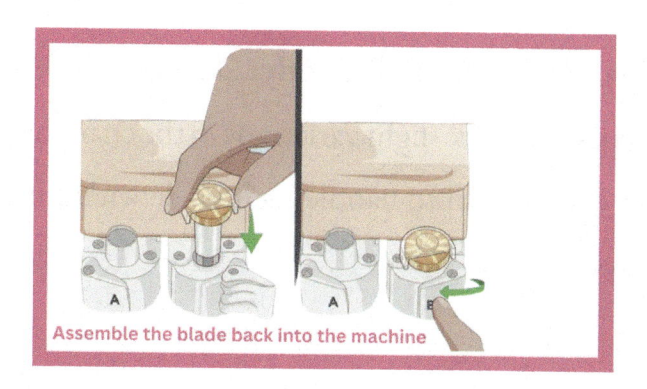

Assemble the blade back into the machine

Caution Changing Cricut Blades:

When changing Cricut blades, it's important to exercise caution to ensure your safety and protect the integrity of the machine. Here are some cautions to keep in mind:

- **Power Off and Unplug:** Before attempting to change the blade, make sure your Cricut machine is powered off and unplugged from the power source. This prevents any accidental activation of the machine during the blade change process.

- **Handle with Care:** Blades are sharp objects, so handle them with caution. Avoid touching the blade edge directly to prevent any accidental cuts. Use tweezers or other tools if needed to safely remove or insert the blade.

- **Handle Blades Differently:** Different models or blade types may have slight variations in the changing process, so it's essential to handle each blade with a unique approach.

- **Use Proper Tools:** Use the recommended tools, such as tweezers or a blade changing tool, provided by the manufacturer. This ensures a secure grip on the blade and reduces the risk of injury.

- **Dispose of Used Blades Safely:** When removing the old blade, handle it carefully to avoid accidental cuts. Dispose of used blades in a sharps container or other appropriate disposal method to prevent injury to yourself or others.

- **Maintain a Clean Workspace:** Ensure your workspace is clear and organized before changing the blade. Removing any potential hazards or distractions will help you focus on the task and prevent accidents.

By taking these cautions into consideration, you can safely and effectively change the Cricut blade, maintaining a smooth and enjoyable crafting experience while prioritizing your safety.

CHAPTER SEVEN
Cricut Materials

Cricut offers a wide range of materials designed for their cutting machines. These materials are crafted to ensure optimal cutting results and compatibility with Cricut machines' capabilities. In this chapter, you learn more about the different Cricut materials.

Cricut materials are designed to deliver optimal cutting results, ensuring clean, precise, and high-quality cuts every time. They are developed with the appropriate thickness, durability, and texture to achieve excellent cutting performance, allowing you to create intricate designs and projects with ease.

Cricut offers a wide range of materials to suit different project needs and creative ideas. Whether you're working with vinyl, cardstock, fabric, iron-on, or specialty materials like leather or foil, Cricut provides options for crafts, and home decor.

Types of Cricut Material:

Here are some of the common types of Cricut materials available:

- Vinyl
- Cardstock
- Iron-On (Heat Transfer Vinyl)
- Infusible Ink Sheets
- Papers
- Fabric
- Adhesive Foil
- Leather
- Acetate
- Poster Board

Vinyl Material:

Vinyl is a widely used and flexible material, perfect for various crafting and DIY projects. It has a thin and adhesive-backed texture that is compatible with the Cricut Maker 3 and other cutting machines.

Different types of vinyl exist, each with unique properties and uses. In this section, we'll provide an in-depth explanation of vinyl material, its various types, the projects you can use it for, and the Cricut Maker 3 blades suitable for cutting it.

Types of Vinyl Material:

Here is a summary of the different types of vinyl material that are available in the market:

- **Adhesive Vinyl:** Vinyl with adhesive is the most popular kind of vinyl available. It has numerous colors, finishes, and adhesive strengths, including permanent and removable. Adhesive vinyl produces decals, labels, personalized home décor, signs, and customizes everyday objects.

- **Heat Transfer Vinyl (HTV):** Heat transfer vinyl, also known as iron-on vinyl, is specially designed to adhere to fabrics using heat. It comes in various colors and finishes, including matte, glossy, glitter, and metallic. HTV is perfect for creating custom T-shirts, tote bags, baby onesies, and other fabric-based projects.

- **Patterned Vinyl:** Patterned vinyl features printed patterns or designs on the surface. It is available in various designs, such as floral, animal prints, geometrics, and more. Patterned vinyl adds a unique and decorative element to your projects, such as laptop skins, home decor accents, or personalized gifts.

- **Permanent Vinyl:** Permanent vinyl has a strong adhesive that creates a long-lasting bond. It is weather-resistant and can withstand exposure to outdoor elements, making it suitable for outdoor signage, car decals, and other projects that require durability.

- **Removable Vinyl:** Removable vinyl is designed to be easily peeled off without leaving any residue behind. It is ideal for temporary applications like wall decals, window decor, and seasonal decorations that you may want to change or remove without damaging the surface.

Vinyl Material

Projects You Can Use Vinyl Material For:

1. **Home Decor:** Vinyl can be used to create wall decals, personalized signs, decorative frames, custom labels, and more to add a personal touch to your living spaces.

2. **Custom Apparel:** With heat transfer vinyl, you can design and customize T-shirts, sweatshirts, hats, and other fabric items with unique designs, monograms, or slogans.

3. **Personalized Gifts:** Vinyl allows you to personalize items such as mugs, tumblers, phone cases, keychains, and more, making them thoughtful and one-of-a-kind gifts.

4. **Party Decorations:** Vinyl can be used to create banners, party favors, cake toppers, and other decorative elements for birthdays, weddings, baby showers, and other special occasions.

5. **Organization and Labels:** Vinyl is perfect for creating labels for jars, containers, files, and other organizational needs, helping you stay organized and adding a touch of style to your space.

Cricut Maker 3 Blades for Cutting Vinyl:

1. **Fine-Point Blade:** The Fine-Point Blade is the standard blade that comes with the Cricut Maker 3 and is suitable for cutting adhesive vinyl, heat transfer vinyl, and patterned vinyl.

2. **Deep Point Blade:** The Deep Point Blade is recommended for cutting thicker vinyl materials or when you need to make deeper cuts, such as when working with thicker adhesive vinyl or certain specialty vinyl.

3. **Bonded-Fabric Blade:** While primarily designed for fabric, the Bonded-Fabric Blade can also be used to cut thin, lightweight vinyl materials effectively.

Vinyl is a versatile material that opens up a world of creative possibilities. With its different types and compatibility with the Cricut Maker 3, you can create personalized and professional-looking projects for various applications.

Cardstock Material:

Cardstock is a commonly used crafting material that is both durable and flexible. It is a heavy paper that comes in a range of colors, textures, and finishes, and is often employed in a variety of creative endeavors.

If you're wondering about the different types of cardstock, the kinds of projects it's suitable for, and which Cricut Maker 3 blades can cut it; this section will teach you about cardstock.

Types of Cardstock Material:

1. **Solid Cardstock:** Solid cardstock is available in various colors and is a basic choice for various projects. It is versatile and works well for creating cards, scrapbooking, paper crafting, and other applications where vibrant and solid colors are desired.

2. **Patterned Cardstock:** Patterned cardstock features printed patterns or designs on the surface, offering a decorative element to your projects. It has various themes, designs, and textures, making it suitable for adding visual interest to cards, scrapbook layouts.

3. **Textured Cardstock:** Textured cardstock has embossed or textured surfaces, adding dimension and tactile interest to your projects. It is available in different textures such as linen, canvas, woodgrain, or embossed patterns. Textured cardstock adds an extra touch of sophistication and uniqueness to your creations.

4. **Specialty Cardstock:** Specialty cardstock includes various specialty finishes, such as glitter, foil, shimmer, or metallic. These specialty cardstocks provide a luxurious, eye-catching look, perfect for special occasions, invitations, and high-end paper crafts.

Cardstock material

Projects You Can Use Cardstock Material For:

1. **Cards and Invitations:** Cardstock is ideal for creating handmade cards, invitations, and announcements. You can cut, score, and fold cardstock to make custom-sized cards and add embellishments or intricate designs using your Cricut Maker 3.

2. **Scrapbooking:** Cardstock is a staple material in scrapbooking. Use it as a base for photo mats, journaling cards, die-cut shapes, and backgrounds. Its durability ensures that your memories are well-preserved.

3. **Paper Crafts:** Cardstock is perfect for various paper crafts, including paper flowers, gift boxes, tags, bookmarks, and party decorations. Its thickness and stability make it easy to manipulate and create three-dimensional designs.

4. **Home Decor:** Use cardstock to create wall art, framed quotes, shadow boxes, and other home decor items. Combine different colors and textures to add a personalized touch to your living spaces.

Cricut Maker 3 Blades for Cutting Cardstock:

1. **Fine-Point Blade:** The Fine-Point Blade is the standard blade that comes with the Cricut Maker 3 and is suitable for cutting most types of cardstock. It provides precise and clean cuts for intricate designs and details.

2. **Deep Point Blade:** The Deep Point Blade is recommended when working with thicker or heavier cardstock, such as heavyweight or specialty cardstock. It allows for deeper cuts and ensures clean results.

3. **Scoring Wheel and Double Scoring Wheel:** The Scoring Wheel and Double Scoring Wheel are essential for creating score lines on cardstock to achieve precise and crisp folds. They are perfect for making cards, envelopes, boxes, and other projects that require accurate scoring.

Iron-On Material (Heat Transfer Vinyl):

Heat Transfer Vinyl (HTV), commonly known as Iron-On material, is vinyl that can be applied to fabrics using heat. It's great for creating custom designs, patterns, and text on fabric projects.

This section provides a detailed explanation of Iron-On material, including its various types, suitable projects, and the appropriate Cricut Maker 3 blades for cutting it.

Types of Iron-On Material (Heat Transfer Vinyl):

1. **Solid Color HTV:** Solid color HTV is the most common type of Iron-On material. It comes in a wide range of vibrant colors, allowing you to create bold and eye-catching designs on fabric.

2. **Glitter HTV:** Glitter HTV adds a touch of sparkle and glam to your designs. It has a textured, glittery finish, giving your projects a dazzling look.

3. **Metallic HTV:** Metallic HTV features a metallic or foil-like appearance, adding a shiny and reflective ele-

ment to your designs. It gives your creations a stylish and sophisticated look.

4. **Flocked HTV:** Flocked HTV has a soft, velvety texture. It adds a unique tactile element to your projects and is often used for creating patches, monograms, and textured designs.

5. **Patterned HTV:** Patterned HTV features pre-printed patterns or designs on the vinyl surface. It eliminates the need for layering multiple colors and patterns and allows you to achieve intricate designs easily.

Iron-On Material

Cricut Maker 3 Blades for Cutting Iron-On Material:

1. **Fine-Point Blade:** The Fine-Point Blade, which comes with the Cricut Maker 3, is suitable for cutting most types of Iron-On material. It provides precise and clean cuts on thin to medium-weight HTV.

2. **Bonded-Fabric Blade:** While primarily designed for fabric, the Bonded-Fabric Blade can also be used for cutting Iron-On material. It is recommended for thicker or textured HTV or when you require more pressure to cut certain Iron-On types.

Iron-On material (Heat Transfer Vinyl) opens up a world of possibilities for customizing fabric items. With its various types and compatibility with the Cricut Maker 3, you can create personalized garments, accessories, and home decor projects with ease.

Infusible Ink Sheets:

Infusible Ink Sheets are a unique heat-transfer material offered by Cricut. Unlike traditional heat transfer vinyl, Infusible Ink Sheets infuse directly into compatible blank materials when subjected to heat.

This results in vibrant, permanent, and professional-quality designs with a seamless and long-lasting finish. Here's an extensive explanation of Infusible Ink Sheets, their types, projects they can be used for, and the Cricut Maker 3 blades suitable for use with Infusible Ink Sheets:

Types of Infusible Ink Sheets:

1. **Solid Color Infusible Ink Sheets:** These sheets come in a wide range of solid colors, allowing you to create bold and vibrant designs on compatible blanks.

2. **Patterned Infusible Ink Sheets:** Patterned Infusible Ink Sheets feature pre-printed designs and patterns, such as florals, geometrics, and more. They offer a quick and easy way to add intricate designs to your projects without the need for complex layering or cutting.

Projects You Can Use Infusible Ink Sheets For:

1. **Apparel:** Infusible Ink Sheets are perfect for customizing T-shirts, hoodies, baby onesies, tote bags, and other fabric items. The vibrant colors and smooth, seamless finish create professional-looking and long-lasting designs.

2. **Home Decor:** You can use Infusible Ink Sheets to personalize coasters, pillow covers, placemats, and other fabric-based home decor items. This lets you add a unique and personalized touch to your living spaces.

3. **Accessories:** Infusible Ink Sheets can be used to create custom designs on accessories like hats, socks, and even shoes. This enables you to express your creativity and style through wearable accessories.

4. **Personalized Gifts:** Infusible Ink Sheets are excellent for creating personalized gifts. You can design and transfer intricate patterns or images onto compatible blanks like mugs, ceramic tiles, and keychains, resulting in customized and one-of-a-kind gifts.

Cricut Maker 3 Blades for Use with Infusible Ink Sheets:

- **Fine-Point Blade:** The Fine-Point Blade, which comes with the Cricut Maker 3, can be used to cut Infusible Ink Sheets. This blade provides precise and clean cuts on the sheets, ensuring accurate transfer of designs onto compatible blanks.

Infusible Ink Sheets offer a unique way to create vibrant and professional-quality heat-transfer designs. With their compatibility with the Cricut Maker 3 and various blank materials, you can unleash your creativity and produce stunning, personalized projects that stand the test of time.

Fabric Material:

Fabric is a versatile material used in sewing, quilting, home decor, fashion, and other textile-related projects. It comes in various types, each offering unique characteristics and suitability for specific applications.

Here's an extensive explanation of fabric material, its types, projects you can use it for, and the Cricut Maker 3 blades suitable for cutting fabric:

Types of Fabric Material:

1. **Cotton:** Cotton is one of the most common and widely used fabrics. It is breathable, soft, and versatile, making it suitable for a wide range of projects such as clothing, quilting, bags, and home decor.

2. **Linen:** Linen is a natural fabric known for its durability, breathability, and elegant drape. It is often used for apparel, home textiles, and table linens.

3. **Denim:** Denim is a sturdy, durable fabric primarily associated with jeans. It is perfect for creating garments,

bags, and accessories that require durability and a casual aesthetic.

4. **Fleece:** Fleece is a soft, warm, and cozy fabric commonly used for making blankets, scarves, hats, and other cold-weather accessories.

5. **Velvet:** Velvet is a luxurious, plush fabric with a soft, smooth texture. It is often used for upholstery, formal wear, and decorative accents.

6. **Satin:** Satin is a shiny, smooth fabric commonly used for evening gowns, lingerie, and elegant home decor items.

7. **Chiffon:** Chiffon is a lightweight, sheer fabric with a soft and flowing drape. It is commonly used for creating feminine garments, scarves, and delicate accessories.

Projects You Can Use Fabric For:

1. **Apparel:** Fabric is commonly used for making clothing items such as dresses, tops, skirts, pants, jackets, and more. The choice of fabric depends on the desired style, comfort, and functionality of the garment.

2. **Quilting:** Fabric is a fundamental component of quilting projects. Quilters use fabric to create intricate patchwork designs, applique elements, and backing for quilts.

3. **Home Decor:** Fabric can be used to create curtains, pillow covers, table linens, upholstery, and other home decor items, allowing you to add a personal touch to your living spaces.

4. **Bags and Accessories:** Fabric is ideal for making bags, tote bags, backpacks, wallets, and various accessories like hats, headbands, and belts.

Cricut Maker 3 Blades for Cutting Fabric:

1. **Rotary Blade:** The Rotary Blade is the recommended blade for cutting fabric with the Cricut Maker 3. It can precisely cut various types of fabric with ease, allowing you to create intricate designs, appliques, and quilt pieces.

2. **Bonded-Fabric Blade:** The Bonded-Fabric Blade is specifically designed for bonded fabrics, where fabric layers are fused together using an adhesive. It can be used for cutting bonded fabrics or lightweight fabrics like organza.

Adhesive Foil:

Adhesive foil is a specialty material that adds a metallic or holographic finish to your projects. It has a self-adhesive backing, making it easy to apply to various surfaces. Adhesive foil is compatible with the Cricut Maker 3 and other cutting machines.

Here's an extensive explanation of adhesive foil, its different types, projects you can use it for, and the Cricut Maker 3 blades suitable for cutting adhesive foil:

Types of Adhesive Foil:

1. **Metallic Adhesive Foil:** Metallic adhesive foil comes in various metallic shades, including gold, silver, copper, and bronze. It adds a luxurious and shiny metallic effect to your projects.

2. **Holographic Adhesive Foil:** Holographic adhesive foil features a mesmerizing, multi-dimensional effect that reflects different colors and patterns when viewed from different angles. It adds a captivating and eye-catching element to your designs.

3. **Patterned Adhesive Foil:** Patterned adhesive foil has printed designs, patterns, or motifs on the surface. It can mimic textures like marble, wood grain, and animal prints or feature intricate geometric patterns. Patterned adhesive foil adds a stylish and decorative touch to your projects.

Projects You Can Use Adhesive Foil For:

1. **Home Decor:** Adhesive foil is perfect for creating custom decorations for your home, such as metallic or holographic wall decals, mirror accents, candle holders, picture frames, or personalized signs.

2. **Party Decorations:** Use adhesive foil to make party banners, cake toppers, party favors, or wine bottle labels. The metallic or holographic finish adds an elegant and festive touch to your celebrations.

3. **Stationery and Cards:** Adhesive foil can be used to embellish cards, envelopes, or stationery items, creating shiny accents, borders, or monograms for a sophisticated and personalized touch.

4. **Custom Apparel and Accessories:** Add a metallic or holographic flair to fabric-based projects by using adhesive foil. Create custom T-shirt designs, tote bags, hats, or accessories like phone cases or keychains.

5. **Crafts and DIY Projects:** Use adhesive foil to add a unique and eye-catching element to various crafts, such as scrapbooking, journaling, paper crafting, or mixed media art.

Cricut Maker 3 Blades for Cutting Adhesive Foil:

1. **Fine-Point Blade:** The Fine-Point Blade, which comes with the Cricut Maker 3, is suitable for cutting adhesive foil. It can handle the thin and flexible nature of adhesive foil, providing clean and precise cuts.

2. **Deep Point Blade:** The Deep Point Blade can be used for cutting thicker adhesive foil materials or when you need to make deeper cuts for more intricate designs.

Adhesive foil offers a glamorous and stylish option for adding metallic or holographic accents to your projects.

Leather:

Leather is a durable and versatile material commonly used in various crafts, fashion accessories, and home decor projects. It is derived from animal hide and is known for its strength, flexibility, and distinctive texture.

Here's an extensive explanation of leather material, its different types, projects you can use it for, and the Cricut Maker 3 blades suitable for cutting leather:

Types of Leather:

1. **Genuine Leather:** Genuine leather is made from the actual animal hide, typically cowhide. It is known for its durability, natural texture, and strength. Genuine leather can come in different finishes, such as full-grain, top-grain, or split leather, each with its own unique characteristics.

2. **Faux Leather:** Also known as synthetic leather or vegan leather, faux leather is a man-made alternative to genuine leather. It is typically made from materials like polyurethane (PU) or polyvinyl chloride (PVC). Faux

leather provides a similar appearance and texture to genuine leather while offering more affordable and cruelty-free options.

Projects You Can Use Leather For:

- **Accessories:** Leather is commonly used to create a wide range of fashion accessories, such as wallets, handbags, belts, keychains, bracelets, and earrings. Its durability and classic look make it an excellent choice for creating stylish and long-lasting accessories.

- **Jewelry:** Leather can be used to make unique and trendy jewelry pieces like necklaces, cuffs, chokers, and earrings. Its versatility allows for various styles, including minimalistic, bohemian, or statement pieces.

- **Home Decor:** Leather adds a touch of luxury and warmth to home decor projects. It can be used to make cushion covers, coasters, wall hangings, plant hangers, or even furniture accents like chair upholstery or drawer pulls.

- **Personalization:** Leather provides an excellent canvas for personalization. You can use it to create personalized keychains, luggage tags, passport holders, or monogrammed leather goods as thoughtful gifts or for yourself.

- **Garments:** Leather is commonly used in the fashion industry for making jackets, vests, skirts, pants, and footwear. It provides a stylish and edgy look and offers protection and durability.

Cricut Maker 3 Blades for Cutting Leather:

1. **Knife Blade:** The Knife Blade is specifically designed for cutting thicker and denser materials like leather. It provides precise and clean cuts, allowing you to create intricate designs or cut leather into various shapes and sizes.

2. **Deep Point Blade:** The Deep Point Blade can also be used to cut thin or lightweight leather effectively. However, for thicker or more intricate leather projects, the Knife Blade is recommended.

When working with leather, it is advisable to use a strong grip or fabric grip cutting mat to secure the leather material in place during the cutting process.

Leather is a versatile and timeless material that adds a touch of elegance and sophistication to your crafts. By using the appropriate Cricut Maker 3 blades and techniques, you can achieve precise and professional-quality cuts, allowing you to bring your leather projects to life with finesse and creativity.

CHAPTER EIGHT
Maintaining Cricut Machine

Maintaining your Cricut Maker 3 is essential to ensure its optimal performance and longevity. Regular maintenance helps keep the machine in good condition and prevents issues affecting its cutting accuracy and overall functionality. This chapter teaches you how to care for and maintain the Cricut machine.

General Care for Cricut Machine:

Here is a general step on how to maintain your Cricut machine:

1. **Clean the Machine:** Use a soft, lint-free cloth or microfiber cloth to wipe down the machine's exterior, removing dust, fingerprints, or any other buildup. Avoid using harsh chemicals or abrasive materials that could damage the machine's surface.

2. **Clean the Blades:** Over time, the blades can accumulate adhesive residue or debris from cutting various materials. To clean the blades, remove them from the blade housing and carefully wipe them with a soft cloth or cotton swab dipped in rubbing alcohol. Ensure the blades are completely dry before reinserting them.

3. **Clear Debris from the Housing:** Occasionally, debris may accumulate in the blade housing. Use a small brush or compressed air to remove any dust or particles that could affect the blade's movement or cutting performance.

4. **Check the Machine:** Inspect the Cricut machine for any signs of damage, wear, or loose parts. If you notice any issues, contact Cricut customer support for assistance or to schedule a repair if needed.

5. **Store Properly:** When not in use, store your Cricut Maker 3 in a clean and dry environment, away from direct sunlight or extreme temperatures. Use the machine's packaging or protective cover to prevent dust accumulation and protect it from accidental damage.

How to Clean Cricut Blades:

The Cricut machine is designed to work with various blades, each specifically crafted for particular materials and cutting needs. A common challenge crafters face is using a blade that has become dull over time.

In such cases, the most effective solution is to replace the blade. However, it's worth noting that debris buildup on the blade could also contribute to its dullness. To address this issue, clean your blade by following the steps below:

- Begin by detaching the blade and its accompanying piece from the tool housing. Gently press the plunger on the blade holder and repetitively insert it into a foil ball. This action helps dislodge any adhered paper or vinyl remnants and can enhance the blade's sharpness.

- To clean the blade area, first remove the attachment and use a stiff-bristled brush to remove any dust. Make sure the bristles reach into the cavity where the blade sits.

- Make sure to use a small amount of canned air to blow into the blade area to remove trapped materials

- After blowing the blade area, wipe everything clean with a dry paper towel.

- The last step is to reattach the blade to the tool housing and the respective clamp.

To increase the lifespan of your blade by up to a year, it's recommended to perform this maintenance routine regularly. It's a good idea to incorporate this technique before and after any projects that involve intricate cuts.

How to Clean Every Part of Your Cricut Machine:

To achieve the best cutting performance, keeping your die-cutting machine clean is essential. Regular cleaning of your Cricut machine is highly recommended to maintain its functionality.

As someone who has owned a Cricut machine for some time, here are some effective cleaning methods that help keep your machine in excellent condition:

Materials Needed:

These are the recommended cleaning essentials that are incredibly useful for cleaning your Cricut machine:

- A roll of absorbent paper towels
- Microfiber cloths or baby wipes
- Canned air

These are the primary material needed, but you can include any other necessary cleaning supplies for your specific needs.

Unplug Cricut:

To ensure a safe working environment, it's important to prioritize safety by first turning off and unplugging your Cricut machine. This should be done before proceeding with any other steps.

Clean the Interior of your machine:

To clean the interior of your Cricut, follow the steps below:

1. Start by accessing the internal components of your machine and releasing the clamps.

2. Remove any blades or tools that may be installed.

3. Get a can of compressed air with a straw attachment to clean precisely.

4. Use short bursts of air to clean effectively, but do not overdo it.

It's essential to also clean the storage trays and be cautious around the caddies and clamps. Remember not to use too much-canned air as it may make the canister colder.

Clean the Clamps:

To clean the clamps individually, use the circular bristle brush. You can also use the same brush to tidy up the Cricut pen adaptor.

Clean the entire machine:

To clean the machine, start by using a baby wipe to wipe down all surfaces, including the inside of the storage trays. Let the machine dry afterwards. Then, use a microfiber cloth to give the machine a final polish and ensure there is no residue left behind from the baby wipes.

Cleaning the rear rod:

It is crucial to avoid disrupting the grease on the back rod, but there might still be some debris that requires removal. To do this, a gentle brushing motion should be used.

Most of the debris is made up of accumulated grease, so brushing it along the rod is recommended to redistribute it. A baby wipe can be used cautiously to get rid of any grease that may have touched the machine near the rod. This process should be repeated on the other end of the rod.

It is recommended to use canned air to remove debris from the teeth at the back of the machine. After cleaning the machine and ensuring it is in a pristine condition, a final once-over with canned air can be done. Move the star wheels back to their original position and close the machine up.

Clean the outside of your Cricut machine:

To keep your machine's exterior clean, use a paper towel with a small amount of liquid cleaner. Be gentle, and don't oversaturate the towel. When cleaning around buttons, be careful not to let any moisture get inside.

To ensure thorough cleaning, use a microfiber cloth to wipe down the entire machine, effectively removing any remaining residue. For hard-to-reach areas, utilize canned air to blow out any debris from cracks and crevices within the machine.

Clean The Back of the machine:

To access the back of the machine, look for an opening at the bottom. Use the round bristle brush to clean any debris in that area. Then, take the canned air and blow it from the front of the machine towards the back to remove any loose debris.

To reinstall the fine point blade, you need to open the machine again. Before doing this, carefully remove the blade from its housing and keep it aside. Use a brush to clean the housing and canned air to clear the blade opening. Wipe the carriage with a dry paper towel.

Once you're done with the cleaning, make sure to put the blade back into the carriage. It's recommended that you wipe it clean using a dry paper towel before doing so. However, if you're cleaning a Cricut Maker, be careful around the adaptive tool system and use canned air for cleaning instead. Other than this, the cleaning process is the same for both types of machines.

How to Clean a Cricut Mat:

Cricut mats are adhesive surfaces used in Cricut machines. They are designed to be used for about 40 times, but with proper cleaning, their lifespan can be extended.

Cleaning a Cricut mat is essential to maintain its stickiness and extend its lifespan. Here's how you can clean your Cricut mat effectively:

1. **Remove Excess Debris:** Gently remove any large debris, such as paper scraps or excess adhesive, from the surface of the mat. You can use a spatula or your fingers to lift off the debris.

2. **Prepare a Cleaning Solution:** Mix a mild liquid soap or dishwashing detergent with warm water in a bowl or sink. Avoid using harsh chemicals or abrasive cleaners, as they can damage the mat.

3. **Clean the Mat:** Dip a soft cloth, sponge, or non-abrasive scrub brush into the cleaning solution. Gently scrub the mat's surface in circular motions to remove any remaining dirt, adhesive residue, or stains. Avoid

using excessive force to prevent damaging the mat.

4. **Rinse the Mat:** Rinse the mat thoroughly under warm running water to remove any soap residue. Ensure that all cleaning solution is completely rinsed off.

5. **Pat Dry or Air Dry:** Use a clean towel or paper towels to pat dry the mat and remove excess moisture. Alternatively, you can let the mat air dry naturally, ensuring it is placed in a flat position away from direct sunlight or heat sources.

6. **Restoring Stickiness:** If the mat has lost some of its stickiness after cleaning, you can restore it by using methods such as applying a light layer of adhesive spray, using a lint roller to remove excess fibers, or lightly dabbing the surface with a baby wipe or rubbing alcohol to rejuvenate the stickiness. Follow the manufacturer's guidelines and recommendations for these methods.

Note: It is important to clean your mat to maintain its stickiness and performance regularly. However, repeated cleaning and exposure to cleaning agents may gradually reduce stickiness.

Author's Note

Dear Valued Reader,

Warm greetings to you! I hope this message finds you thriving and full of literary enthusiasm. As a self-publishing author, I write to you today with a humble request for a review of this book.

Behind every book lies a tale of devotion—a testament to the countless hours poured into its creation. My dedicated team and I have spared no effort in meticulously gathering and curating the wealth of information encapsulated within these pages.

Dear valued reader, we aim to provide you with a valuable collection of insightful information, thorough research, and practical knowledge regarding your Cricut Machine. We invested both money and time into creating this book.

Therefore, your feedback holds immeasurable value in our journey. Please take a few moments to leave a review on Amazon. Click on this **Link** or visit (*www.amazon.com/review/create-review?&asin=B0CCMSTXLQ*) to rate this book.

Your comments will tell us how well we perform and guide fellow readers from the extensive wisdom we have painstakingly compiled. We are eagerly awaiting to hear your thoughts and insights. Thank you for considering our request. We appreciate your review and comments, and we will keep them in mind.

CHAPTER NINE

Cicut Design Space: Introduction

Cricut Design Space is a web-based software application developed by Cricut that allows users to design, customize, and create projects for their Cricut cutting machines. In this chapter, you will learn about the software.

Cricut Design Space is the primary software in Cricut, used to create and manipulate designs before sending them to the Cricut machine for cutting, drawing, or writing.

Cricut Design Space provides a user-friendly interface with various design tools and features, including text editing, image upload and editing, shape manipulation, layering, and various design effects.

Why Cricut Design Space:

Cricut Design Space plays a crucial role in the Cricut ecosystem and offers numerous benefits and importance for users of Cricut cutting machines. Here's an extensive explanation of the importance of Cricut Design Space:

1. **Design and Customization:** Cricut Design Space provides a robust platform for designing and customizing projects. It offers various design tools, including text editing, shape manipulation, layering, image upload and editing, and different design effects. Users can create unique, personalized designs that suit their preferences and project requirements.

2. **User-Friendly Interface:** Design Space features a user-friendly interface that is intuitive and easy to navigate. It allows users to quickly learn and utilize the software, regardless of skill level. The interface provides a streamlined workflow, making it accessible for beginners while still offering advanced features for more experienced users.

3. **Extensive Design Library:** Design Space offers a library of pre-designed images, fonts, and projects. This library provides users with a wealth of creative content, allowing them to find inspiration and easily incorporate high-quality designs into their projects. The vast design library saves time and effort by eliminating the need for users to create designs from scratch.

4. **Image and Font Upload:** Design Space allows users to import their own images and fonts, providing limitless possibilities for customization and personalization. This feature enables users to work with their own unique designs, logos, or handwritten fonts, ensuring that their projects reflect their individual style and creativity.

5. **Project Accessibility and Synchronization:** Design Space is a web-based software accessible through a web browser or mobile app. This cloud-based nature allows users to access their projects from different devices and locations, providing flexibility and convenience. Designs created on one device are automatically synced and accessible on other devices.

6. **Machine Integration and Compatibility:** Cricut Design Space seamlessly integrates with Cricut cutting machines. It provides a direct connection between the software and the machine, allowing users to set cut and draw parameters, choose materials, and send their designs for precise cutting or drawing. Design Space supports various Cricut machines, ensuring compatibility and ease of use.

7. **Regular Updates and New Features:** Cricut continuously updates and improves Design Space, introducing new features, design content, and enhancements. These updates expand the creative possibilities for users, ensuring they have access to the latest tools, functionalities, and design options. Regular updates also improve the software's performance, stability, and user experience.

In summary, Cricut Design Space is a vital component of the Cricut experience. It empowers users to unleash their creativity, customize projects, and bring their unique designs to life with ease.

Install Cricut Design Space For iPad/iPhone:

To download and install Cricut Design Space on your iPhone or iPad, follow these steps:

1. **Open the App Store:** Tap the App Store icon on your device's home screen.

2. **Search for Cricut Design Space:** In the App Store's search bar, type "Cricut Design Space" and tap the search button.

3. **Select the Cricut Design Space App:** From the search results, find the official Cricut Design Space app and tap on it to open the app page.

4. **Check Compatibility:** Ensure your device meets the minimum requirements for running Cricut Design Space. The app should be compatible with your iPhone or iPad version and operating system.

5. **Get/Download Icon:** On the app page, tap the "**Get**" button or the cloud icon with a downward arrow to initiate the download and installation process. You may

be required to enter your Apple ID password or use Touch ID/Face ID for verification.

6. **Wait for the Download to Complete:** Allow the app to download and install on your device. The progress will be indicated by a downloading circle on the app icon.

7. **Open Cricut Design Space:** Once the installation is complete, locate the Cricut Design Space app on your home screen and tap on it to launch the app.

8. **Sign In or Create an Account:** If you already have a Cricut account, sign in using your credentials. If not, create a new account within the app.

9. **Start Designing:** Once you're signed in, you can start exploring Cricut Design Space, accessing your projects, and creating new designs right from your iPhone or iPad.

NOTE: Make sure your device is connected to the internet during the download and installation process. Ensure that you have enough storage space on your device for the app.

Frequently Asked Questions (FAQ):

Below are frequently asked questions about Cricut Design space and the answers to alleviate users' concerns about the software.

Is an internet connection required to use Design Space?

Yes, an internet connection is required to use Design Space. Design Space is a web-based software, and it relies on an internet connection to access and sync your designs, fonts, and projects.

The internet connection allows you to access the extensive design library, utilize cloud storage for your projects, and take advantage of the software's online features and functionalities.

While you can work on projects offline using the Design Space app on compatible mobile devices, an internet connection is needed to save, sync, and transfer your designs between devices and to send projects to your Cricut machine for cutting or drawing.

Connecting to the internet ensures seamless integration and synchronization between Design Space and your Cricut cutting machine, providing a smooth and efficient crafting experience.

Which Cricut machines can be used with Design Space?

Design Space is compatible with a range of Cricut cutting machines, including the following models:

- Cricut Maker
- Cricut Explore Air 2
- Cricut Explore Air
- Cricut Explore One
- Cricut Joy

These machines can be connected to Design Space via a USB cable or wirelessly using Bluetooth technology. It's important to ensure that both the machine and Design Space are updated to the latest firmware and software versions for optimal compatibility and performance.

Does Design Space Support multiple computers and mobile devices?

Yes, Cricut Design Space can be used on multiple computers and mobile devices. Design Space is a cloud-based software allowing users to access their projects and designs from various devices.

Whether you're using a desktop computer, laptop, tablet, or smartphone, you can log in to your Design Space account and access your projects seamlessly. The software synchronizes your projects across devices, ensuring that any changes or designs you create on one device are automatically updated and accessible on other devices.

This flexibility allows you to work on your Cricut projects from different locations and devices, providing convenience and accessibility. Just make sure to download the Design Space app from the App Store (for iOS devices) or visit the Design Space website (for computers) to log in and continue your creative journey across multiple devices.

CHAPTER TEN
Design Space: Canvas Overview

Imagine the Design Space canvas as your own creative playground, where you can turn your ideas into stunning designs. On this platform, you can create new projects, add images and text to your existing work, and perfect them until they meet your expectations.

The Canvas:

The software's main work area is called the canvas. At first, it might seem confusing and too much to handle, but the more you use it, the easier it will become to understand the various icons, buttons, and options on the screen. Additionally, you can use this book as a helpful guide to assist you in your journey.

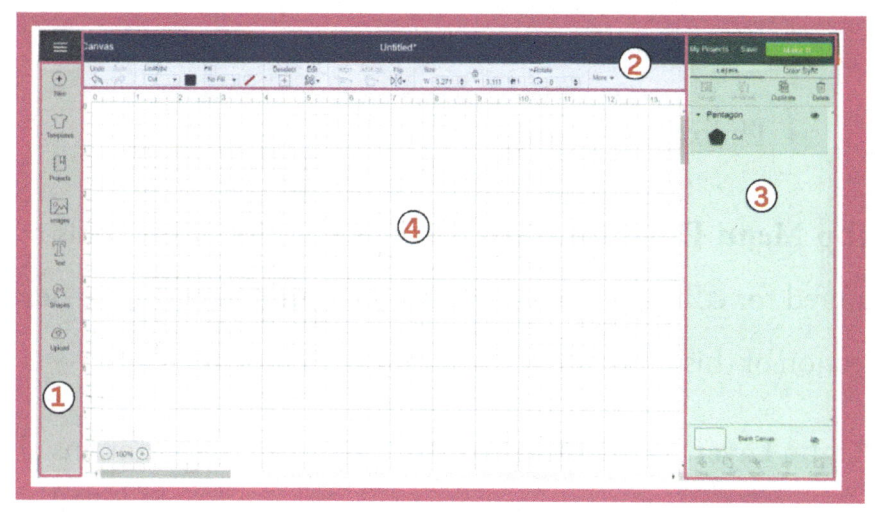

Design Space Canvas

To help you understand better, I've divided the canvas screen into four different sections, as shown above.

Left Panel (Marked 1): This contains the main insert area with all the functions, such as

- New

- Templates

- Projects

- Images

- Text

- Shape

- Upload

Top Menu Panel (Marked 2): The majority of the tools required for editing your project can be found here. In the next section of this book, we will examine each tool in detail.

Right Layer Panel (Marked 3): The layer panel contains all the objects, shapes, images, and text in your design, each of which has its own layer. The layer panel updates as you add more elements to your design, showing you the layers associated with each added element. (We'll cover this topic in more detail in upcoming chapters).

Center Canvas Area (Marked 4): The canvas area is where your design will come to life. This is the section with gridlines, as shown in the screenshot above. Throughout this guide, I will walk you through the four main sections of the canvas, explaining each icon, button, and option.

The Left Panel:

The left panel of Cricut Design Space is a prominent and essential element of the software's interface. It offers a range of tools, features, and options that facilitate the design and customization process. Here's an overview of the components typically found in the left panel:

New:

On the left panel, the first option (New) is to start a new project. Clicking it will give you an empty canvas. If you're already working on a project and click "**New**," a pop-up will ask if you want to save your current work or replace it with a new canvas.

Template:

To access templates for your design, click on the second tool on the left panel of your canvas. This will bring up a screen with numerous templates that can help you visualize how your design will appear on a surface.

Template

You can select a template that matches what you want to create and use it as a guide to developing your own design. For example, if you want to add text to your shirt, you can select the shirt template, adjust the size and dimensions, and type in the text. Once you have added your text, place it where you want it to be on the shirt.

TIP: Although the templates cannot be saved or cut out, they are a great tool to help you visualize and set up the size, dimension, space, and other properties of your design.

Starting a project does not require a template, but a template is the perfect visual aid if you want to see how your design will look on a surface.

To adjust the size of a template, select it and look for the size options in the top left panel. Once the template is loaded onto the canvas, you can find the 'Type,' 'Size,' and 'Color' options just above the canvas area. Use these options to customize the template to your liking.

Projects:

One of the best features in design space is the 'Projects' option. It provides you with a variety of design projects that are already created for you. This means that you don't have to be an expert in design to create a stunning design.

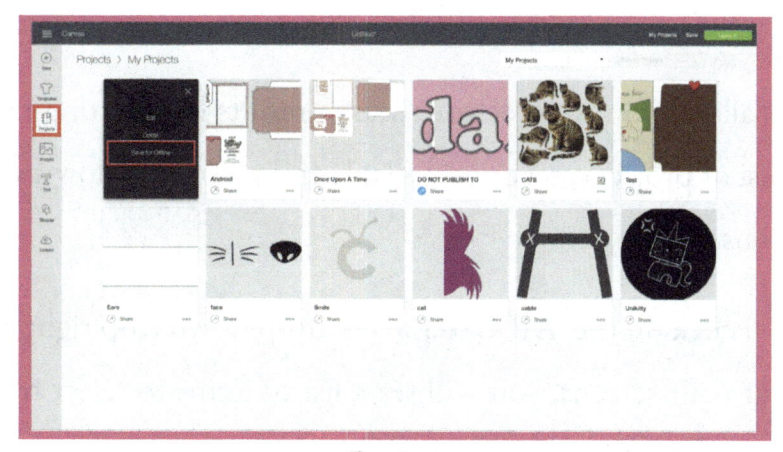

Projects

To access pre-designed projects, click on the '**Project**' icon. From there, you can scroll through and select any design you prefer.

Note: It's important to know that not all projects are free. Some require a purchase, but you can access most projects as a Cricut access member. Look for the projects with an 'A' sign on a little green banner, as those are available with your subscription.

If you don't have a Cricut Access subscription, you can still make a one-time purchase of any project you're interested in. Once you've made the purchase, you'll be able to use the design as many times as you want, whenever you want.

If you're new to this Design Space, I suggest you explore the available free projects. To find them, click the drop-down button at the top right of the Project screen.

This allows you to filter your search results by selecting from the list of project categories available and narrowing down your options.

If you click on the '**All Categories**' drop-down (top right corner of your screen), you will see a list of items to select from. They are simply inexhaustible.

Images:

On the left panel, there is an option called 'Images.' This tool helps add pictures to your design. For instance, if you want to create a tablecloth with a teddy bear image, you can click on the 'Image' icon and browse through the images displayed to find a suitable teddy bear picture for your design.

You can use the drop-down search button at the screen's top right corner if you prefer a more specific search. Type in what you are looking for, such as a teddy bear, in the provided space. Additionally, you can search for images by selecting the 'Categories' option at the screen's top right corner.

Text:

Moving down the line is the 'Text' tool. This is a very important tool with much functionality. It may take you a while to master everything about this tool; however, it becomes easier with time and practice.

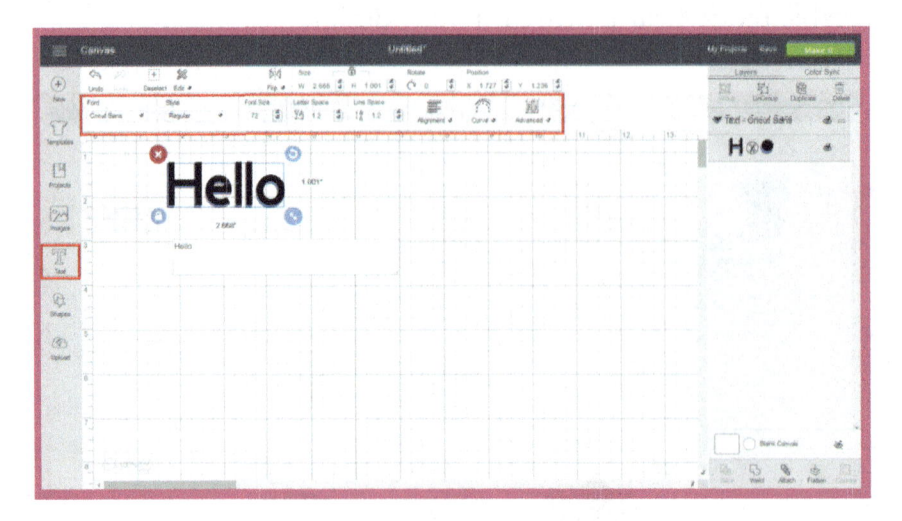

The first thing you will notice when you click on the 'Text' tool is a blank work area with a text box. You type your text in the box, which is seen on the blank canvas. In the screenshot above, I typed in 'Hello World.'

The second thing you will notice is that the top menu panel contains the Text edit menu, which is a function needed to edit your text. In the text edit panel, you can change the font of your text.

Click on the font icon, and you will see several styles of font you can select from, including Cricut fonts and system fonts (fonts installed on your PC). You will also find other text editing attributes to set how you want your text to appear in your design.

These options include font size, line and letter spacing, alignments, and so on. The key to using these tools is the downward and upward pointing arrows. So, if you want to decrease the font size of a text, you simply hit the down arrow.

On the other hand, if you want to increase the font size, you hit the up arrow until you are satisfied with the result. This rule applies to most of the text editing tools. (Much of these text attributes are covered in the next section of this book).

Another useful text editing tool is the 'Isolate Layer' button. This is used for isolating a letter from a text, giving you the ability to edit that letter separately. So, you can choose to increase the size of a single letter, change the font style, rotate it, and so on.

The easiest way to isolate the letters in a text is to select the text on the canvas, right-click on the mouse, and select the 'Ungroup' button from the drop-down.

Now you can work on each letter individually, customizing them as you like. When you are satisfied with the outcome, you may need to regroup the letters so you can work (move, edit, rotate, etc.) on the text as a whole. To do this, select the text, right-click on the mouse button, and click '**Group**.'

Shape:

The shape tool allows you to add shapes to your design. You can choose from a selection of different shapes to experiment with; square, circles, heart shape, star shape, triangle, etc.

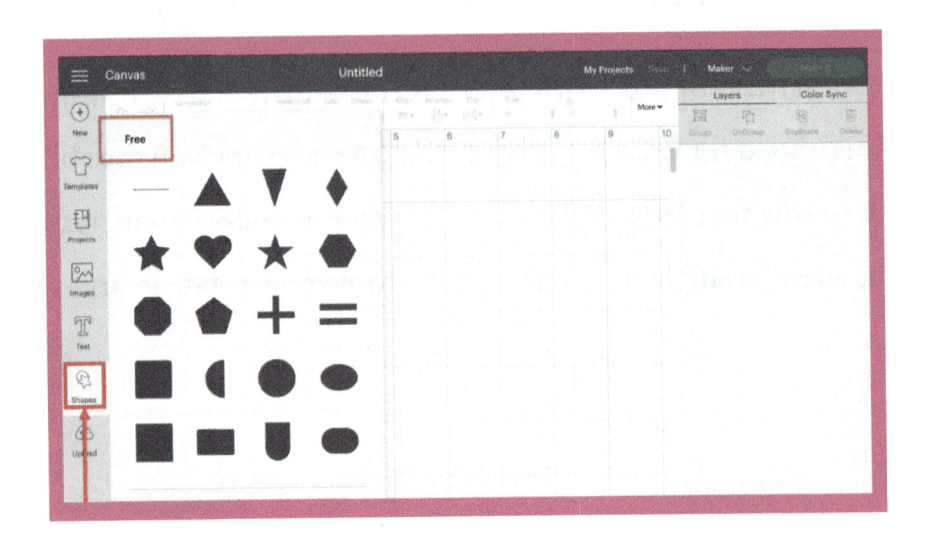

The exciting thing about working with shapes is the ability to customize them. You can add/change colors, add patterns, adjust the size, rotate them, etc. The possibilities are endless, as you will see later on in this book.

Upload:

This is the last tool on the left panel of the canvas. When you click on it, it takes you to a screen where you can upload designs or images on your system to cut them with your Cricut. You could also get many pre-made designs from the internet, upload them into design space and cut them.

Assuming you already have a design or shape on your canvas, you'll notice four different icons at the four corners of the selected element. The first icon at the top left edge is an 'x' sign that you can use to close the shape or element at any time.

On the shape/design's lower left edge, a padlock icon can be used to keep the element's proportions intact while resizing. If you wish to resize without maintaining proportions, click on the padlock to unlock it.

CHAPTER ELEVEN

Design Space: Top / Editing Bar

To better understand the Top Bar in Design Space, it's important to define some key terminologies first. Please be aware that some of the terminology used in this guide are commonly used computer tools that should be easy to understand.

However, everyone's level of computer literacy may vary. Therefore, pardon me if you already know many of them. This has been done for the sake of those who do not know. The terms are as follows:

Undo/Redo:

This icon is used to reverse any change made to the layer or redo any previously taken undone action.

Linetype:

This icon indicates how the machine will interact with the material on the mat, such as cut, draw, and score, on your material.

- **Cut:** The Cut line type involves using a blade to cut through a layer of material. It is used when you want to precisely cut out shapes or designs from your material, allowing you to create intricate and detailed cuts.

- **Draw:** The Draw line type utilizes a Cricut pen instead of a blade. It instructs the machine to draw along the designated path, adding decorative elements, handwritten text, or intricate patterns to your project.

- **Score:** The Score line type creates indentations or creases on your material without cutting through it completely. It is typically used for folding lines in projects such as cards, boxes, or other items that require clean and precise folds.

- **Engrave:** The Engrave line type is designed for engraving, allowing you to create engraved designs or patterns on compatible materials.

- **Deboss:** The Deboss line type is used to create depressions or indentations on compatible materials, giving your designs a raised, textured effect. Debossing adds dimension and tactile appeal to your projects.

- **Wave:** The Wave line type, also known as the wavy line, creates a decorative wavy pattern along the designated path. It adds a fluid and dynamic element to your designs, enhancing the overall visual appeal with its flowing and undulating effect.

- **Perf:** The Perf line type, short for perforation, creates a series of small, evenly spaced holes along the designated path. It allows for easy tearing or separation of sections in projects like tear-away cards, coupons, or detachable elements.

- **Foil:** The Foil line type is specific to certain Cricut machines and tools designed for foiling. It enables you to add metallic or decorative foils to your designs, creating eye-catching accents or patterns on compatible materials.

These line types in Cricut Design Space offer a range of capabilities, allowing you to choose the appropriate method to achieve the desired outcome in your projects.

Linetype Swatch:

When creating a layer, you can choose additional attributes to use. The options available depend on the type of line chosen (cut, draw, or score).

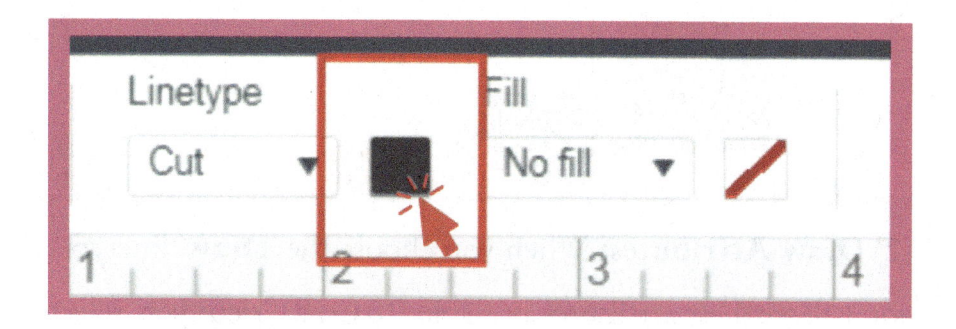

(1) **Cut Attributes:** These are the available attributes that will show up when the '**Cut**' linetype is selected. The options available for cut attributes are;

- **Material colors:** To match project colors effortlessly, simply select your preferred shade from the Material colors palette. Once selected, a checkmark will appear in the color swatch for the chosen layer.

- **Advanced:** To choose a color, you can slide the bar in the custom color picker or manually enter the hexadecimal code of your desired color.

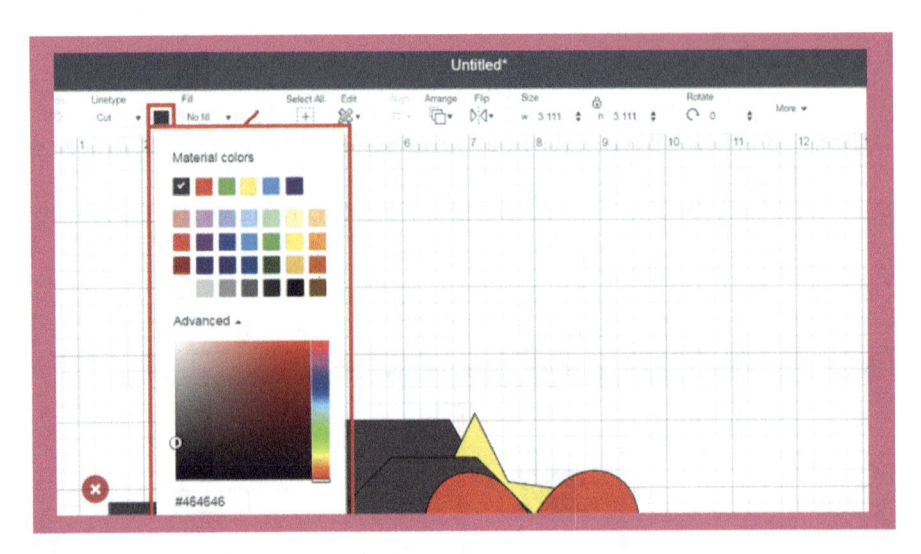

(2) **Draw Attributes:** When you choose the '**Draw**' linetype, you will see these attributes available. To use a Cricut pen, select

it from the drop-down menu. The list of available colors will vary based on the type of pen you choose.

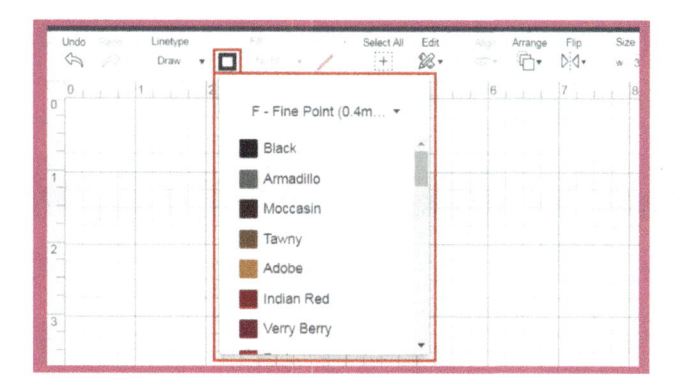

Fill:

This is used to fill the image layers for printing with the chosen color or pattern.

- **No Fill:** This is used to cut the layer without filling the image layer. Therefore, it can be used to change the layer to 'Cut' only after applying '**Fill**.'

- **Print:** This is used to access color and pattern options when using '**Print and Cut.**"

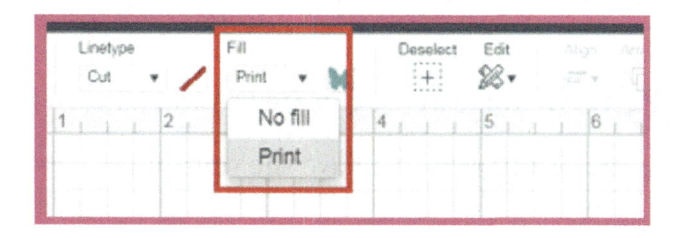

Fill Swatch:

This is used when you intend to choose additional 'Fill' attributes for the image layer, including color and patterns for 'Print Then Cut' images.

Fill attributes: Suppose you Select Print in fill; you will need to select a color or pattern fill for the image.

- **Original Artwork:** This option is used to restore a 'Print' layer to its original state, thereby removing any editing work you do.

- **Color:** This is used to select the 'Print then Cut' color from the basic color palette, custom color picker, current material colors, or inputting the hex color code.

- **Pattern:** You can use this tool to add pattern fill to text layers or images. You have the option to narrow down your search for patterns by filtering the color. Once you have found the desired pattern, you can use the 'Edit Pattern' tools to adjust its scale and orientation within the image.

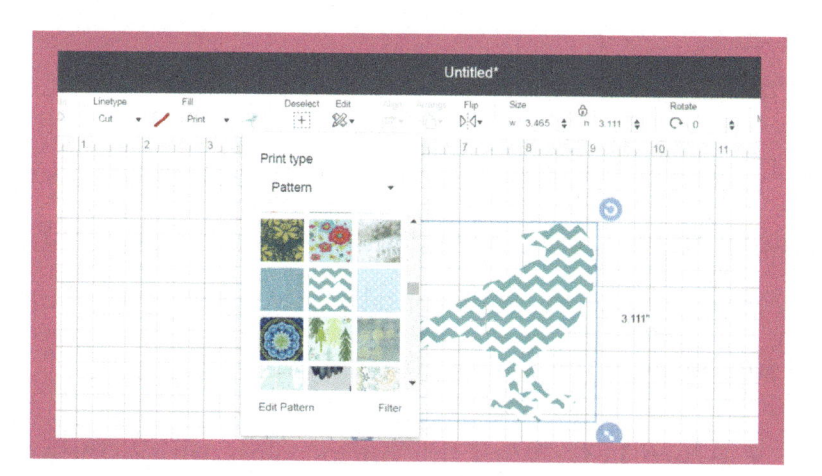

Select All/Deselect:

To select or deselect all items on the canvas at once, use this option.

Edit:

This is used to find normal editing tools, including cut, copy and paste. Use the Cut option to remove an image from the clipboard to paste later; The Copy option is used to copy an image; The Paste option is used to paste a copied or cut image from the clipboard onto the canvas.

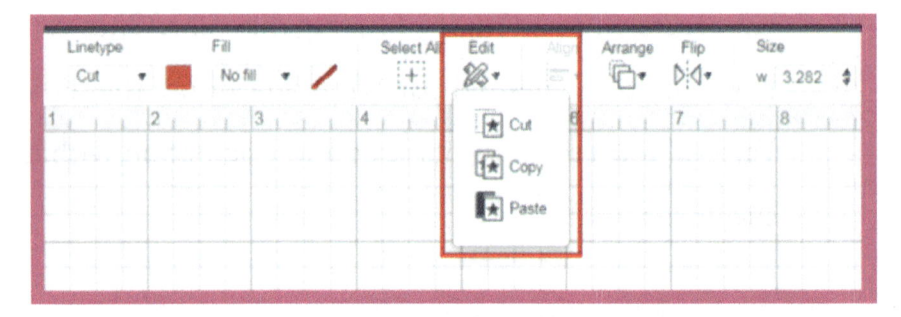

Align:

This is used to position two or more images/objects using a defined margin. You can line up the images to the left, right, top or bottom, and center (horizontally or vertically). Under this tool are some options as described below.

- **Align Left:** With this option, you can position two or more images/objects using the left margin. The leftmost edge of the object on the canvas feels its effect.

- **Align Right:** With this option, you can position two or more objects using the right margin. The right-most edge of the right-most object of the selected feels the effect of this option when you click it.

- **Align Top:** This option positions images/objects using the top margin. The topmost edge of selected objects/images will feel its effect.

- **Align Bottom:** With this option, you can position two or more images/objects using the bottom margin, and the bottom-most edge of the bottom-most selected objects will feel its effect.

- **Center:** This option is used to line up all the central points of the selected objects. It is also used to stack images on top of each other.

- **Center Horizontally:** This defines the horizontal center point of two or more objects/images, and its effect is felt by the exact horizontal center of selected images/objects (the central point).

- **Center Vertically:** This option is used to position two or more images/objects using the vertical center margin. The central point will be the exact vertical center of the selected objects/images, where its effect will be felt when you click this option.

- **Distribute Horizontally:** You can position the selected images to be evenly distributed between the left and right edges of the objects that you selected.

- **Distribute Vertically:** This option is used to position the selected objects to be evenly distributed between the topmost and bottom-most edges of the objects that you selected.

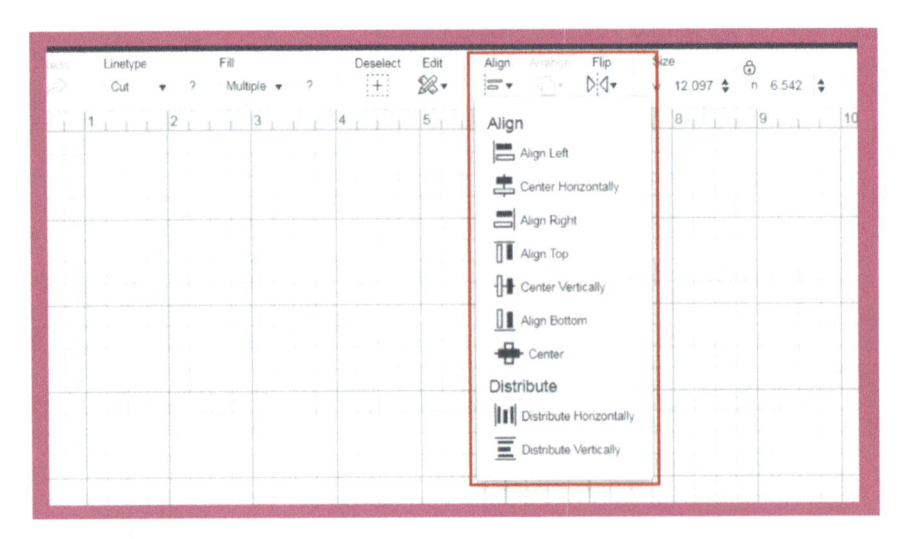

Arrange: You use this feature to adjust the arrangement of objects on the Canvas by using the options to Move to Back, Move Backward, Move to Front, and Move Forward. Any changes you make will be shown in the Layers Panel.

- **Send to Back:** Like the name, it is used to send the selected object to the back of the stack according to the order of stacking. Therefore, the object will move to the bottom of the Layers Panel.

- **Move Backward:** This option moves the selected object one layer to the back according to the stacking order.

- **Move Forward:** With this option, you can move the selected object one step (layer) forward according to the stacking order. Therefore, the object moves one layer forward in the 'Layers Panel.'

- **Send to Front:** This moves the selected object to the front according to the stacking order. This will make the object appear at the top of the Layers Panel.

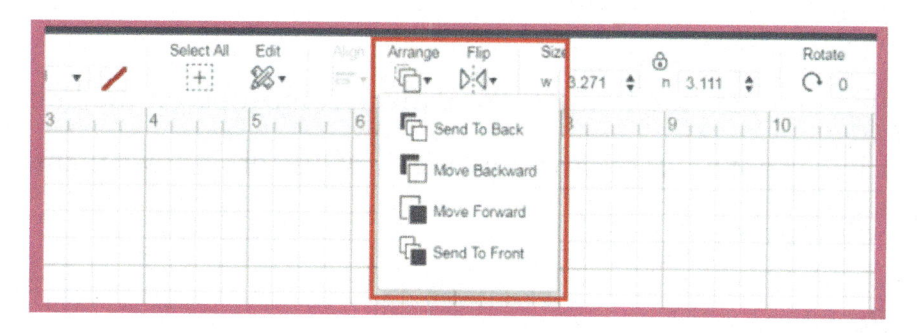

Flip:

This feature is used to flip an object horizontally or vertically.

- Flip Horizontal: To flip an object horizontally, place the center of the object as the pivot point.

- Flip Vertical: Flip an object vertically at the center of the object.

Size:

If you need to change the size of an object, you have two options. You can enter a specific value for its width or height or use the stepper to make adjustments in 0.1 increments.

Rotate:

To adjust the angle of your object, you can either enter an exact degree or use the stepper to adjust it by one degree at a time.

More:

If your screen resolution is too narrow, some tools on the Edit bar may not be visible. In such cases, a "More" drop-down menu will appear.

Position:

To adjust the position of your object, you can either enter an exact distance from the top left corner of the Canvas or use the stepper to adjust the distance by increments of 0.1.

Placing Text or Images on Design Screen:

To change the linetype, go to the 'Edit' bar and click on the 'Linetype' drop-down. The current linetype will be highlighted.

If you want to change the linetype of multiple layers, select the layers and choose the desired linetype from the drop-down. Your selection will be reflected in the canvas image once you have made the change.

To utilize the 'Print then Cut' option, click on the 'Fill' drop-down and choose 'Print.' Select 'Color' or 'Pattern' from the 'Fill' swatch drop-down if you want to include a color or pattern in the layer.

When using the 'Write' or 'Score' linetype in a project with multiple layers, it is necessary to attach the image to another layer. To do this, select both layers in the 'Layers' panel and click the 'Attach' button.

How to Perform Linetype from Android/iOS

- To begin, add your text or images to the design screen.

- Then, navigate to the Layers panel by tapping on the 'Layers' button at the bottom of the screen.

- Once you are in the Layers panel, click the arrow next to the layer to access the 'Layer Attributes' panel.

- You will see that the current linetype is highlighted. Choose the linetype you want by tapping on it.

- Finally, if you have finished selecting your linetype, tap on the 'Layers' button again to close the panel.

Working with Fonts in Design Space:

Cricut Design Space offers a unique feature of personalizing projects with distinct fonts and text. This feature allows you to express your creativity freely, tapping into your innate creative ability. The satisfaction and sense of accomplishment of delivering projects to your taste are unparalleled.

Cricut Design Space has an incredible feature that allows you to change the font even after ungrouping or isolating letters. You can use either the Cricut fonts or those installed on your computer or device.

Let's explore how to add text, select fonts, and install/uninstall them on Windows/Mac, one step at a time.

Adding Text to Cricut Design Space:

To access the 'Text' tool, go to the left-hand side of the canvas. If you're using the iOS or Android app, you'll find it at the bottom-left of the screen.

Once you've selected the text tool, iOS/Android users will see the font list appear, while Windows/Mac users will see the text bar and text box appear.

Please choose the font size and type that you would like to use before inputting your text. If you want to start a new line within the same textbox, press the "Return" key after typing out the previous line.

How to Edit Text in Cricut Design Space:

You can adjust the text's size, placement, and even rotation. Here's an easy guide to editing text on the canvas.

Editing text is a straightforward process—Double-click on the text to reveal the available options. From there, you can choose the action you want to perform, including changing the font style.

Using the Edit bar, you can adjust the font type, font size, letter spacing, and line spacing. The Edit bar is found at the top of the canvas for Windows/Mac users and at the bottom of the canvas for iOS/Android users.

How to Select Fonts:

If you are familiar with the 'Image Edit Tool,' then you will easily navigate the 'Text Edit Tool' in Cricut Design Space.

The reason for their similarity is that both tools operate similarly by rotating, sizing, and positioning text. This similarity is helpful as it simplifies the task of editing text and finding the appropriate font. As a result, it becomes easier to personalize projects.

Are you familiar with the bounding box? If not, let me explain. The bounding box is the rectangular outline that surrounds your selected text. It serves as a boundary for the text box and has round handles on each corner. These handles allow for easy text editing, such as rotating, resizing, deleting, and locking or unlocking the aspect ratio.

In Cricut Design Space, the Edit bar allows you to customize the features of specific images or text. These features include linetype, size, rotation, fill, positioning, and mirroring. You can also adjust line spacing, font styles, and letter spacing when working with text layers. If you're wondering how to edit the font, I can guide you through the process.

To edit a text object on the canvas, select it. You can also insert text from the design panel or choose a text layer from the 'Layers Panel.' Once selected, the 'Text Edit Bar' will appear below the 'Standard Edit Bar.' Keep in mind that the 'Standard Edit Bar' will disappear when you're not interacting with the text.

Font Filter:

You can select your preferred font type from the options available in the 'Font Type' menu, categorized by different categories. There are various font filters available, which are explained further below.

- **All Fonts:** This displays all the available fonts for you.

- **System Fonts:** This display the fonts found on your computer.

- **Cricut Fonts:** This displays fonts from the Cricut library.

- **Single-Layer Fonts:** These display fonts containing just one layer.

- **Writing Style Fonts:** This display specifically designed fonts that are written with a pen.

Style:

You can choose from various font styles, such as italic, bold, regular, bold italic, and writing style. Please keep in mind that the available style options may vary depending on whether you are using a Cricut font or a System Font.

Font Size:

This option allows you to alter the size of the font using the point size. You can type the point size value or use steppers to change the value incrementally.

Letter Space:

This allows you to alter the space between letters. Like the font size, you can type in the value or use the steppers.

Line Space:

This enables you to change the spacing between rows of text. Again, you can type in the value or use the steppers, as discussed previously.

Alignment:

This allows you to position the entire block of text to the left, right, or center, or even full justification.

Curve:

This enables you to bend the text into a circular shape. This is a good option for a crafter who designed write-ups for curved materials, such as tumblers, bowls, and buckets.

CHAPTER TWELVE
Design Space Tips

Design Space in Cricut is like a spice that adds flavor to your design in the Cricut, and it's one of the most important tools for getting the most out of your Cricut machine. Here are a few tips that will be useful;

How to use Color Sync Panel

In Cricut Design Space, the Color Sync panel allows you to match the colors of your project to a specific color palette or brand. To use the Color Sync panel:

- Open the project you want to work on in Cricut Design Space.

- Select the "*Canvas*" tab on the right side of the screen.

- Click on the "*Color Sync*" panel, which is located in

the "Layers" section of the right sidebar.

- In the Color Sync panel, you will see a list of the colors used in your project, as well as a list of color palettes and brands that you can choose from.

- Select the palette or brand from the list to match the colors in your project to a specific color palette or brand.

- Cricut Design Space will automatically update the colors in your project to match the selected palette or brand.

- If you want to customize the colors in your project, you can click on any of the colors in the Color Sync panel to open the color picker and choose a different color.

- When you're finished, click "***Apply***" to save your changes.

How to Use Patterns in Cricut Design Space

Pattern is a feature used to fill any text or image layers in Cricut Design Space. It is important to know that there are numerous patterns in the Cricut Design Space pattern library. If you do not like any of the patterns, you can customize or upload your own pattern. Here is how to use patterns;

- Open the project you want to work on in Cricut Design Space.

- Select the "*Canvas*" tab on the right side of the screen.

- Click on the "*Layers*" panel in the right sidebar.

- In the Layers panel, select the layer that you want to apply a pattern to.

- Click on the "*Fill*" dropdown menu in the Layers panel, and select "*Pattern.*"

- A list of available patterns will appear. Scroll through the list and select the pattern you want to use.

- The pattern will be applied to the selected layer.

- If you want to customize the pattern, click on the "***Customize***" button next to the pattern name. This will open the Pattern Options panel, where you can adjust the size, alignment, and orientation of the pattern.

- When you're finished, click "***Apply***" to save your changes.

How to Mirror Designs

During the heat transfer process, your iron-on design will be protected by the shiny, clear, heat-resistant liner that is attached to most iron-on materials. Your machine can only cut your pattern if the liner is facing down. Consequently, before you begin cutting, you'll want to make a mirror image of your design in Design Space. Here is how to go about the process;

- Once you have finished customizing your design and are ready to cut, click on the "***Make It***" button to proceed to the project preview.

- If you have any design elements intended for heat transfer, make sure to toggle the "***Mirror***" switch on for each load type. Then, click "***Continue***" to complete your cut.

- If you forget to mirror your design and select a heat-transfer material setting, Design Space will remind you to do so. To fix this, click "**Edit**" and toggle the "***Mirror***" switch on, then select "**Done**." Repeat this process for each load type as needed.

- Once you have finished these steps, you are ready to cut your design.

Working with Text in Design Space

For new text to be added to Canvas, click the Text icon. A text box with the word "Text" highlighted. The text is in edit mode when it appears like this. To update your text, begin to type.

How to Modify Text:

The Edit mode ends if you click anywhere other than the text field, but making changes is simple;

- Double-click on your text, and choose Edit Text from the menu to add new words or make edits.

- Another option is to use the Edit menu's feature, or by right-clicking within the text box, you may cut, copy, and paste while the letter(s) are chosen.

How to Rotate Text

You can rotate the text box on a canvas by using any corner handle of a bounding box or by entering a number in the Rotate input field in the Edit toolbar.

Allow the pointer to hover slightly beyond the corner handle of the bounding box while rotating until a curving arrow emerges. Rotate the text by clicking and dragging.

Sizing a Text

Text may be resized by dragging any corner handle on the bounding box or by entering values in the Size input boxes on the Edit toolbar. In the Edit toolbar, click the Lock symbol next to the width and height fields to unlock proportions so you may separately alter the width and height.

Resizing the text box

You don't have to modify the font size you've chosen to change the size of the box your text is in. Click and move the bounding box's main rectangular handles. By default, the text is aligned horizontally and vertically, but you may change the position of the text inside the text box by using the Alignment, Letter Space, and Line Space tools.

Text Wrapping

By default, just one line of text is put to the canvas. No line breaks are necessary; depending on the size of your text box, you may have your text wrap or flow to a new line.

Click and drag a center rectangular handle on the text box to move a word to a new line or bring a word back from the previous line. Your text box enters wrap mode as a result. Select Wrap Off from the Alignment menu to get out of the Wrap mode.

How to Curve Text

You may shape-shift your text into a circle with the Curve tool. To discover how to curve text in Design Space, go to this help page.

How to Delete Text

Use the delete keys on the keyboard to remove text.

Design Space Tricks

Here are a few tips and tricks for using Cricut Design Space:

- Use the "**Duplicate**" option to create multiple copies of an object quickly. This is especially useful for creating repeating patterns or for making small adjustments to multiple copies of the same object.

- Use the "**Group**" and "**Ungroup**" options to manipulate multiple objects as a single unit. This is useful for moving and resizing multiple objects at once.

- Use the "**Align**" and "**Distribute**" options to quickly and easily align multiple objects. These options allow you to align objects by their edges and centers or evenly distribute them across a page.

- Use the "**Weld**" option to merge two or more shapes into a single object. This is useful for creating more complex shapes or for combining text and images.

- Use the "**Contour**" option to cut out a shape or design from a larger object. This is useful for creating intricate cuts or for creating a "negative" version of a shape.

- Use the **"Flip"** option to quickly and easily reverse an object horizontally or vertically. This is useful for creating mirrored images or adjusting an object's orientation.

- Use the **"Fill"** and **"Outline"** options to add color to your designs. The Fill option allows you to add color to the inside of an object, while the Outline option allows you to add color to the outline of an object.

- Use the **"Layers"** panel to organize your designs and keep track of which objects are on top or behind others. This is especially useful for creating multi-layered designs or for adjusting the visibility of different objects.

CHAPTER THIRTEEN

Turning Hobby Into Business With Cricut Maker 3

Turning your beloved hobby into a full-time business is a dream many passionate individuals share. Imagine spending your days doing what you love, pursuing your creative interests, and having the opportunity to share your talents with the world while earning a living.

The Concept of Work:

In this fast-paced and ever-evolving world, the concept of work is evolving too. More people are seeking fulfilment and purpose in their professional lives, moving away from the traditional nine-to-five grind to pursue their passions.

The digital age has opened up avenues for creative entrepreneurs to connect with a global audience, showcase their talents, and turn their hobbies into profitable businesses.

Whether it's crafting, writing, designing, or any other hobby that brings you joy, the possibility of transforming it into a successful venture is within reach.

However, the transition from hobbyist to full-time entrepreneur requires careful planning, dedication, and a strategic approach. It involves understanding your target market, refining your skills, developing a business plan, and effectively marketing your offerings.

It's about recognizing the value of your craft, finding your unique selling point, and creating a brand that resonates with your audience.

This journey is not without challenges, but the rewards are immeasurable. The ability to wake up excited about your work every morning, pour your heart and soul into your creations, and witness their positive impact on others is an incredible feeling.

It offers the freedom to shape your own destiny, pursue your passions on your terms, and build a sustainable business that reflects who you are.

Can I Turn My Craft into a Profitable Business?

Absolutely! The Cricut Machine is a powerful tool to help you turn your craft into a profitable business. Its cutting capabilities, with a wide range of compatible materials, open up endless possibilities for creating unique, personalized products that resonate with customers.

Here is why the Cricut Maker 3 can be instrumental in launching and growing a profitable business and make money:

Product Diversification: The Cricut Machine allows you to work with various materials, including vinyl, cardstock, fabric, leather, and more.

This versatility enables you to offer various products, from customized apparel and accessories to home decor, party supplies, personalized gifts, and more.

Creating diverse and high-quality products allows you to attract a larger customer base and tap into different market segments.

Online Selling Opportunities: The rise of e-commerce platforms and online marketplaces provides a global reach for selling your craft.

You can showcase your products on your website, social media platforms, and online marketplaces like Etsy or Shopify.

With visually appealing product images and compelling descriptions, you can attract customers from around the world and take advantage of the growing demand for handmade and unique items.

Customization and Personalization: One of the standout features of the Cricut Maker 3 is its ability to create customized and personalized products.

Customers today value unique and individualized items that reflect their personal style or commemorate special occasions.

With the Cricut Maker 3, you can easily incorporate names, monograms, special messages, or custom designs into your products, offering a personalized touch that sets you apart from mass-produced alternatives.

Professional-Quality Finishing: The precise cutting capabilities of the Cricut Maker 3 ensure clean and professional finishes for your products.

Whether it's intricate designs, intricate patterns, or precise shapes, the machine delivers consistent and precise results that elevate the quality of your craft. This level of professionalism can enhance the perceived value of your products, making them more appealing to customers.

Community and Support: The Cricut community is vast and supportive, with numerous online forums, groups, and tutorials available to help you learn, grow, and connect with fellow crafters and entrepreneurs.

Sharing your work, seeking inspiration, and collaborating with others in the community can provide valuable insights, mentorship, and networking opportunities that contribute to the success of your business.

Starting A Cricut Business:

Turning your hobby into a successful business with the Cricut Maker 3 can be an exciting and fulfilling journey. Here is an extensive exploration of the steps on how to transform your hobby into a thriving business:

Identify Your Niche: The first step is to identify your niche market. Determine the specific products or services you want to offer.

The Cricut Maker 3 offers many possibilities, including customized apparel, personalized home decor, party supplies, paper crafts, and more. Focus on an area where your skills and interests align, ensuring you can deliver high-quality, unique products or services.

Research and Validate Your Market: Conduct thorough market research to understand your chosen niche's demand, competition, and potential customers.

Identify your target audience, their preferences, and pricing expectations. This research helps you tailor your offerings and marketing strategies to meet the needs of your target market.

Develop a Business Plan: Create a detailed business plan that outlines your goals, target market, products or services, pricing, marketing strategies, financial projections, and operational considerations.

A well-crafted business plan provides a roadmap for your business, helps secure funding if needed, and serves as a reference to track your progress and make necessary adjustments.

Build Your Brand: Establish a strong brand identity that reflects your unique style, values, and offerings.

Develop a compelling brand name, logo, and visual elements that resonate with your target audience.

Consistently apply your brand across all touchpoints, including packaging, marketing materials, social media, and your online presence.

Create a Portfolio of Products: Utilize the Cricut Maker 3 to create a diverse product portfolio that showcases your skills and attracts customers.

Experiment with various materials, designs, and techniques to offer various options. High-quality and eye-catching products will help establish your reputation and generate interest in your business.

Perfect Your Craft and Technique: Continuously refine your skills and stay up-to-date with the latest trends, techniques, and design possibilities offered by Cricut Maker 3.

Experiment with different materials, blades, and tools to unlock the machine's full potential. This dedication to mastering your craft will set you apart and enable you to offer unique, high-quality products that customers will value.

Create a Strong Online Presence: Establish an online presence through a website or e-commerce platform to showcase your products and reach a wider audience.

Utilize social media platforms like Instagram, Pinterest, and Facebook to share your work, engage with potential customers, and build a community around your brand. Regularly update your online platforms with visually appealing content and product highlights.

Pricing and Profitability: Determine your pricing strategy based on factors such as material costs, labor, competition, and market demand.

Ensure that your pricing covers expenses and allows for a reasonable profit margin. Regularly assess your costs and adjust pricing as needed to maintain profitability while remaining competitive in the market.

Marketing and Promotion: Develop a marketing strategy that includes both online and offline channels to reach your target audience.

Utilize social media marketing, search engine optimization (SEO), content marketing, influencer collaborations, and email marketing to create brand awareness, drive traffic to your website, and generate sales. Participate in local craft fairs, trade shows, or community events to gain exposure and connect with potential customers in person.

Scale and Diversify: As your business grows, explore opportunities to scale your operations.

Consider hiring help, outsourcing certain tasks, or investing in automation tools to increase productivity and meet growing demand. Explore new product lines, collaborations, or partnerships to diversify your offerings and expand your customer base.

Choosing Your Cricut Clientele:

Choosing your Cricut clientele is crucial to running a successful business with your Cricut machine. Identifying and targeting the right audience can help you tailor your products, marketing strategies, and customer experience to meet their specific needs and preferences.

Here are some key considerations and strategies to help you choose your Cricut clientele effectively:

Identify Your Niche: Start by defining your niche market within the broader Cricut community. Determine the specific type of products you want to create and the audience that is most likely to be interested in them.

For example, you can specialize in personalized wedding decor, children's accessories, or customized home organization solutions. By focusing on a niche, you can position yourself as an expert and develop a strong brand presence.

Research Your Target Market: Conduct thorough market research to understand your potential customers. Identify their demographics, interests, purchasing behavior, and preferences.

Look for trends and patterns within your niche to uncover opportunities for product development and marketing strategies.

Social media platforms, forums, and online communities related to crafting and Cricut can provide valuable insights into the needs and desires of your target audience.

Analyze Competition: Study your competitors within your niche to better understand the market landscape. Analyze their products, pricing, marketing strategies, and customer feedback.

This analysis can help you identify gaps or areas where you can differentiate yourself and offer unique value to your potential customers. It's important to find a balance between standing out from the competition and still addressing the desires of your target audience.

Define Your Ideal Customer: Create a detailed profile of your ideal customer, also known as a buyer persona. Consider factors such as age, gender, lifestyle, interests, and purchasing power.

Determine their motivations, pain points, and aspirations. This persona serves as a guide to tailor your products, messaging, and marketing efforts to resonate with your target audience. It helps you communicate directly to your ideal customer, making your marketing efforts more effective.

Craft Compelling Marketing Messages: Once you clearly understand your target market, develop marketing messages that speak directly to their needs and desires. Highlight your products' unique benefits and features that resonate with your audience.

Use language, visuals, and storytelling techniques that connect emotionally with your target customers. Craft compelling product descriptions, social media captions, and website content that evoke value and inspire them to engage with your brand.

Utilize Social Media and Online Channels: Leverage the power of social media and online platforms to reach and engage with your target audience. Identify the platforms that your ideal customers frequent the most and establish a strong online presence there.

Share high-quality visuals of your products, provide valuable content related to your niche, and actively engage with your audience through comments, messages, and discussions. Build relationships and community around your brand to foster customer loyalty.

Gather Customer Feedback: Regularly seek feedback from your customers to understand their experience, preferences, and areas for improvement.

Use surveys, reviews, and direct communication channels to gather insights that can help you refine your products and enhance the customer experience. Customer feedback is invaluable for making informed decisions and adapting your business to better serve your clientele.

Remember, choosing your Cricut clientele is an ongoing process that requires continuous evaluation and adaptation. As you grow your business and gain more insights, you may refine your target market and adjust your strategies accordingly.

Stay connected with your customers, be open to feedback, and consistently deliver exceptional products and experiences to build a loyal customer base and drive the success of your Cricut business.

Tips For Making Money and Setting Cricut Business:

Here are some tips to help you make money and set up a successful Cricut business:

Identify Profitable Products or Services:

1. Research the market to identify profitable products or services that align with your skills and interests.

2. Consider trends, customer demand, and competition in your chosen niche.

3. Look for unique angles or gaps in the market that you can fill with your Cricut creations.

Develop a Strong Brand Identity: Create a cohesive brand identity that reflects your unique style and values. Choose a compelling business name, design a professional logo, and establish consistent visual elements across your marketing materials and products. A strong brand identity helps you stand out from competitors and build brand recognition.

Define Your Target Audience:

Identify your target audience and understand their preferences, needs, and purchasing behaviors. This will help you tailor your products, pricing, and marketing messages to reach and engage your ideal customers effectively. Consider factors like age, interests, lifestyle, and demographics to refine your target audience profile.

Price Your Products Strategically:

1. Determine pricing that is competitive yet profitable for your Cricut products.

2. Consider factors such as material costs, labor, overhead expenses, and market demand.

3. Conduct market research to assess the pricing of similar products in your niche.

4. Factor in your time and expertise when setting your prices.

Develop a Marketing Strategy:

1. Create a comprehensive marketing strategy to promote your Cricut business.

2. Utilize both online and offline channels to reach your target audience.

3. Leverage social media platforms, craft-related forums, local craft fairs, and word-of-mouth referrals to increase your visibility.

4. Use compelling visuals, engaging content, and effective storytelling to showcase your products and connect with potential customers.

Build an Online Presence:

1. Establish an online presence through a website or e-commerce platform to showcase and sell your Cricut products.

2. Optimize your website for search engines to increase your online visibility.

3. Utilize social media platforms to share your work, engage with followers, and drive traffic to your website.

4. Create valuable content related to your niche to attract and retain your target audience.

Offer Customization and Personalization: Capitalize on Cricut's ability to offer customization and personalization. Personalized products can differentiate your business and attract customers seeking unique and unique items. Offer customization options like names, monograms, or specific designs to cater to individual preferences.

Provide Excellent Customer Service:

1. Deliver exceptional customer service to build customer loyalty and generate positive word-of-mouth.

2. Respond promptly to inquiries, address concerns, and ensure timely delivery of orders.

3. Strive for excellence in every customer interaction to foster long-term relationships and repeat business.

Stay Updated and Evolve:

1. Stay current with Cricut trends, new materials, and techniques to keep your offerings fresh and relevant.

2. Attend workshops, join online communities, and participate in industry events to network and learn from others.

3. Embrace new technologies, adapt to customer feedback, and continuously improve your skills and processes.

Manage Finances Wisely:

1. Keep track of your business expenses, revenues, and profits.

2. Set aside funds for materials, equipment maintenance, marketing efforts, and business growth.

3. Maintain accurate records and consult an accountant or financial advisor to ensure proper financial management.

Seek Growth Opportunities:

1. As your Cricut business grows, explore opportunities to expand your offerings or reach new markets.

2. Consider collaborations, wholesale opportunities, or create complementary products.

3. Continuously assess the market and adapt your business strategies to stay ahead of the competition and maximize growth potential.

Building a successful Cricut business takes time, effort, and dedication. Stay passionate, continually improve your skills, and strive for excellence in every aspect of your business.

With the right mindset and strategic approach, you can turn your Cricut hobby into a profitable venture that brings joy to both you and your customers.

CHAPTER FOURTEEN
Selling Your Craft

Selling your Cricut craft creations can be an exciting and rewarding way to share your creativity with the world while earning an income.

The Cricut machine empowers you to design and produce a wide range of personalized and unique items that resonate with customers seeking handmade and customized products.

Whether you're passionate about crafting home decor, personalized apparel, party supplies, or personalized gifts, turning your Cricut craft into a profitable business venture offers endless possibilities.

This chapter will explore the ins and outs of selling your Cricut craft, providing valuable insights and practical tips to help you navigate this exciting entrepreneurial journey.

Where can I sell my Cricut Craft?

There are numerous platforms and avenues to sell your Cricut craft creations. Here are some popular options to consider:

- Online Marketplaces

- Social Media Platforms

- Website or Online Shop

- Craft Fairs and Local Markets

- Consignment Shops and Boutiques

- Custom Orders and Commissions

When deciding where to sell your Cricut craft creations, consider your target audience, fees and commissions involved, the level of competition, and the platform's policies regarding handmade items.

Online Marketplaces:

Selling your Cricut craft creations in online marketplaces like Etsy, Amazon Handmade, and eBay offers a fantastic opportunity to reach a wide customer base and establish your brand in the online crafting community.

These platforms provide dedicated marketplaces for handmade and artisanal products, making them ideal for showcasing and selling your unique Cricut craft items. Here is an explanation of each online marketplace to sell your Cricut craft:

Etsy:

- Etsy is one of the most popular and well-established platforms for selling handmade and vintage items. It has a large and dedicated customer base specifically looking for unique, handmade products.

- Setting up an Etsy shop is relatively easy and allows you to create a personalized storefront to showcase your Cricut craft creations. Add high-quality product photos, detailed descriptions, and pricing information.

- Etsy provides various tools and features to help you optimize your shop, such as keyword tags, customizable policies, and the ability to offer product customisation options.

- The platform also offers promotional opportunities like running sales, participating in seasonal events, and utilizing social media integrations to boost your visibility and attract customers.

- Etsy charges listing and transaction fees on sales, so it's important to factor these costs into your pricing strategy.

Amazon Handmade:

- Amazon Handmade is a section of Amazon dedicated to handmade and artisanal products. It provides access to a massive customer base and offers the trust and credibility associated with the Amazon brand.

- Creating an Amazon Handmade Seller account allows you to list and sell your Cricut craft items alongside other handmade products.

- The platform offers features like personalized storefronts, enhanced brand pages, and the ability to leverage Amazon's fulfilment network for order processing and shipping.

- Amazon Handmade charges a referral fee on each sale, and there are specific guidelines and requirements for product eligibility and quality.

eBay:

- eBay is a widely recognized online marketplace that allows you to list and sell various products, including your Cricut craft creations.

- Setting up an eBay seller account allows you to choose between auction-style listings or fixed-price formats for your Cricut items.

- eBay provides tools and features to help you optimize your listings, including detailed descriptions, pricing options, and various promotional options to attract buyers.

- The platform offers a large customer base and international selling opportunities, allowing you to reach a broader audience for your Cricut craft items.

- eBay charges various fees, including listing fees, final value fees, and additional fees for optional features or upgrades. It's important to understand and factor in these costs when setting your prices.

When selling on these online marketplaces, it's crucial to optimize your product listings with high-quality images, detailed descriptions, and relevant keywords to improve visibility and attract potential buyers.

Additionally, customer service plays a significant role in building trust and receiving positive feedback. Promptly respond to customer inquiries, process orders efficiently, and ensure timely shipping of your Cricut craft items.

Social Media Platforms:

Selling your Cricut craft creations through social media platforms can effectively reach a wide audience, engage with potential customers, and grow your business. Here's an explanation of the different social media platforms you can sell your craft:

Facebook Marketplace:

- Facebook Marketplace provides a convenient platform to sell your Cricut craft items locally. It allows you to create listings with detailed descriptions and high-quality product photos and set prices for your creations.

- Start by creating a dedicated Facebook page for your business, where you can showcase your Cricut craft creations, share behind-the-scenes content, and engage with your audience.

- Optimize your listings by including relevant keywords, clear descriptions, and accurate categorization. Use compelling visuals that highlight the unique features of your products.

- Leverage the power of local selling by targeting customers in your area. Utilize location filters and include specific pickup or delivery details in your listings.

- Engage with potential customers by promptly responding to inquiries, addressing concerns, and providing additional information about your products. Encourage customer reviews and testimonials to build trust and credibility.

Instagram:

- Instagram is a visual-centric platform that allows you to showcase the aesthetic appeal of your Cricut craft creations. Create an Instagram business account specifically for your Cricut business.

- Post high-quality photos and videos of your products, utilizing relevant hashtags to reach a wider audience. Experiment with different styles, compositions, and settings to create visually engaging content.

- Engage with your followers by promptly responding to comments, direct messages, and inquiries. Foster a sense of community by sharing user-generated content and featuring customer testimonials.

- Utilize Instagram Stories and Highlights to provide sneak peeks, behind-the-scenes glimpses, and exclusive offers. Utilize the "Shop" feature to tag your products and enable direct purchasing from your posts.

- Collaborate with influencers, craft-related accounts, or complementary businesses to expand your reach and gain exposure to your followers.

Twitter:

- Twitter offers a platform to engage in real-time conversations, share updates, and promote your Cricut craft business. Create a Twitter account dedicated to your business.

- Share visually appealing photos of your Cricut craft items and engaging captions highlighting their unique features, uses, or customization options.

- Utilize relevant hashtags related to crafting, Cricut, and your specific niche to increase visibility and attract relevant followers.

- Engage with the crafting community by participating in relevant Twitter chats, replying to tweets, and sharing valuable content. Retweet and engage with influential accounts and industry leaders to build connections and expand your reach.

- Share updates on new product launches, promotions, and upcoming events. Encourage customer feedback and respond to inquiries and comments promptly.

Regardless of your social media platform, consistency, authenticity, and engaging content are key. Regularly update your profiles, interact with your audience, and provide value through educational content, tutorials, and inspirational ideas.

Utilize features like live videos, polls, and giveaways to drive engagement and foster a loyal community. Remember to include links to your website or online shop to facilitate easy purchasing.

Your Own Website or Online Shop:

- Create your own website or set up an e-commerce platform to sell your Cricut craft creations. Platforms like Shopify, WooCommerce, or Squarespace provide user-friendly options for building an online store and managing your inventory and sales.

Craft Fairs and Local Markets:

- Participate in local craft fairs, markets, or community events to showcase and sell your Cricut craft items. These events provide an opportunity to interact with customers, receive immediate feedback, and build local connections.

Consignment Shops and Boutiques:

- Approach local consignment shops, boutiques, or gift stores that align with your target market and inquire about the possibility of consigning or selling your Cricut craft items through their retail space.

How Should I Price My Cricut Item?

Pricing your Cricut items appropriately is essential to ensure profitability, cover costs, and position your products competitively in the market. Here are some key factors to consider when determining the pricing for your Cricut items:

Calculate Costs:

1. Begin by calculating the costs associated with creating each Cricut item.

2. Consider the cost of materials, such as vinyl, paper, or fabric, and any additional supplies like adhesive, thread, or embellishments.

3. Factor in the cost of Cricut blades, machine maintenance, and packaging or shipping materials.

Evaluate Time and Labor:

1. Assess the time and effort required to create each item.

2. Consider the design process, cutting time, assembly, and any additional customization or finishing touches.

3. Determine an hourly rate that reflects your skills and expertise, and estimate the labor cost for each item accordingly.

Research Market Prices: Research the market to understand the price range of similar Cricut items. Analyze competitor pricing on online marketplaces, craft fairs, and local stores. Avoiding underpricing your items while being competitive is important, as it can undervalue your craft and profitability.

Consider Unique Value: Consider the unique value your Cricut items offer compared to mass-produced alternatives. You can justify a higher price point if your products feature intricate designs, personalization options, or high-quality finishes. Emphasize the craftsmanship and attention to detail that comes with handmade and personalized items.

Target Audience and Demand:

1. Evaluate your target audience and their willingness to pay for your Cricut items.

2. Consider their preferences, purchasing power, and perceived value.

3. Adjust your pricing strategy accordingly to align with your target market's expectations.

Profit Margins: Determine the profit margin you aim to achieve for each item. This should account for your costs and a reasonable return on investment. Consider allocating a portion of the profit towards business growth, marketing efforts, and future material investments.

Pricing Strategy: Choose a pricing strategy that aligns with your business goals. Options include:

- Cost-Plus Pricing: Add markup to your total costs to determine the selling price. This ensures you cover all expenses and generate a profit.

- Competitive Pricing: Set your prices based on the market average or slightly below or above your competitors. Consider the unique value you bring to justify any higher pricing.

- Value-Based Pricing: Set prices based on the perceived value your Cricut items offer to customers. This approach focuses on your products' benefits, uniqueness, and customization options.

Testing and Adjusting:

1. Test your initial pricing strategy and observe how customers respond.

2. Monitor sales, customer feedback, and profit margins.

3. If necessary, be open to adjusting your prices based on market trends, customer preferences, or changes in your cost structure.

Remember, pricing is not a static decision. Regularly reassess your pricing strategy based on market conditions, competition, and the value you provide. Striking the right balance between profitability, customer satisfaction, and market competitiveness is key to running a successful Cricut business.

Should I Quit My Day Job?

Deciding whether or not to quit your day job to pursue a full-time Cricut business is a significant decision that requires careful consideration. Here are some factors to contemplate when making this choice:

Financial Stability: Evaluate your current financial situation and determine if you have enough savings or alternative income sources to sustain yourself during the initial phases of your Cricut business.

Consider the potential income you can generate from your Cricut business and weigh it against your current salary and financial obligations.

Market Demand and Business Growth: Assess the market demand for your Cricut products and evaluate the growth potential of your business. Conduct market research, analyze competitor performance, and consider the overall viability of your business idea.

If there is strong demand and growth potential, transitioning to full-time entrepreneurship may be more feasible.

Business Performance and Stability: Evaluate the performance and stability of your Cricut business. Look at your sales, customer feedback, and overall business trajectory.

If your business is consistently generating revenue, has a loyal customer base, and shows signs of sustainable growth, it may indicate that it has the potential to support you full-time.

Risk Tolerance: Consider your personal risk tolerance. Starting a full-time Cricut business involves inherent risks and uncertainties.

Assess your ability to handle the financial risks, market fluctuations, and potential setbacks that may arise when relying solely on your business for income.

Work-Life Balance and Passion: Assess your personal goals, values, and desired work-life balance. Determine if pursuing your Cricut business full-time aligns with your long-term aspirations and brings you fulfilment.

Consider the challenges and sacrifices of being self-employed, including potential long hours and the need for self-motivation.

Transition Plan: Develop a transition plan to ensure a smooth shift from your day job to full-time entrepreneurship.

Consider factors such as establishing a financial buffer, building a solid customer base, and creating a comprehensive business plan to guide your transition.

Support System: Evaluate your support system, including friends, family, or mentors who can provide guidance and assistance during your entrepreneurial journey. Having a strong support system can help you navigate challenges and provide emotional and professional support.

Ultimately, quitting your day job and pursuing your Cricut business full-time is highly personal and depends on your unique circumstances, goals, and risk tolerance.

Start your Cricut business as a side hustle initially, gradually scaling it up and testing the waters before making a final decision.

CHAPTER FIFTEEN
Cricut Project Idea

The Cricut machine offers crafters a treasure trove of project possibilities that can bring your imagination to life, from personalized gifts and home decor to stunning apparel, intricate paper crafts, and a lot more.

In this chapter, we will embark on a journey through a myriad of Cricut project ideas that will inspire your inner artist and ignite your passion for crafting. You will also discover unique ways to use different materials and experiment with various Cricut blades.

Leather Cuff Bracelet:

Leather cuff bracelets have become a popular statement piece, adorning the wrists of both men and women.

Creating a leather cuff bracelet allows people to express their unique style, embrace individuality, and make a fashion statement that reflects their personality.

Materials Needed:

- Genuine leather or faux leather

- Cricut Maker 3 machine

- Standard Grip Mat

- Fine Point Blade

- Cricut Design Space (computer or mobile device)

- Weeding tools

- Leather adhesive or strong glue

- Snap fasteners or other closure options

- Scissors

Step 1: Designing in Cricut Design Space

- Open Cricut Design Space on your computer or mobile device and create a new project.

- Measure the width and length of your leather strip and input the dimensions into Design Space.

- Browse the design library or create your own custom design for the bracelet. Adjust the size, position, and orientation as desired.

- Once satisfied with the design, proceed to the "Make" screen and ensure that the cut settings are set to "Leather" or "Custom" with appropriate settings for your specific leather type.

- Connect your Cricut Maker 3 to your computer or mobile device, load the fine point blade, and place the leather strip on the standard grip mat.

Step 2: Cutting the Design

- Follow the on-screen prompts in Cricut Design Space to ensure proper mat loading and calibration.

- Press the "Start" button in Design Space to begin cutting the design. The Cricut Maker 3 will precisely cut out the desired shape and details from the leather strip.

- Once the cutting is complete, unload the mat from the machine and carefully remove the leather pieces from the mat, using weeding tools if necessary.

Step 3: Assembling the Bracelet

- Apply leather adhesive or strong glue to the backside of the cut leather pieces, ensuring even coverage.

- Align the pieces according to the design, carefully pressing them together to create the desired bracelet shape. Follow the adhesive manufacturer's instructions for drying time.

- Use a leather hole punch or rotary punch to create holes for the closure. Ensure they are evenly spaced and sized to accommodate the chosen closure mechanism.

- Attach the snap buttons or closure of your choice to secure the bracelet ends.

Step 4: Finishing Touches

- Trim any excess leather from the edges of the bracelet using scissors or a rotary cutter, creating clean and even edges.

- Optionally, you can personalize the bracelet further by adding additional embellishments, such as metal studs, embroidery, or decorative stitching.

Step 5: Applying Transfer Tape (optional)

- If your design includes intricate details or layered elements, apply transfer tape over the design to help transfer it onto the leather more easily.

Congratulations! You have successfully created a stylish men's leather cuff bracelet using Cricut Design Space and the Cricut Maker 3. Feel free to experiment with different leather types, colors, and designs.

Cosmetic Bag:

Cosmetic bags are essential for organizing and storing beauty and skincare products, making them popular and in demand.

You can combine functionality with personalized style by creating a custom cosmetic bag using Cricut Design Space and the Cricut Maker 3. Whether for personal use or as thoughtful gifts, handmade cosmetic bags offer a unique touch that stands out in the market.

Materials Needed:

- Cotton or canvas fabric (main fabric and lining)
- Fusible interfacing
- Zipper

- Cricut Maker 3
- FabricGrip mat
- Rotary cutter or fabric scissors
- Sewing machine
- Iron and ironing board
- Pins or fabric clips
- Sewing thread

Step 1: Designing in Cricut Design Space

- Open Cricut Design Space on your computer or mobile device and start a new project.
- Browse the design library or create your own custom design for the cosmetic bag. Adjust the size and shape according to your preferences.
- Measure the dimensions of the bag you want to create and input them into Design Space. Ensure the design fits within the desired size.

- Once satisfied with the design, proceed to the "**Make**" screen and ensure that the cut settings are set to "Fabric" or "Custom" with appropriate settings for your fabric type.

- Connect your Cricut Maker 3 to your computer or mobile device, load the FabricGrip mat, and place the fabric on the mat.

Step 2: Cutting the Fabric Pieces

- Follow the on-screen prompts in Cricut Design Space to ensure proper mat loading and calibration.

- Press the "**Start**" button in Design Space to begin cutting the fabric pieces. The Cricut Maker 3 will accurately cut out the fabric shapes for the cosmetic bag.

- Once the cutting is complete, unload the mat from the machine and carefully remove the fabric pieces, ensuring they are not distorted or stretched.

Step 3: Preparing the Fabric

- Iron the fabric pieces to remove any wrinkles and ensure

they lay flat.

- Apply fusible interfacing to the fabric pieces following the manufacturer's instructions. This helps add stability and structure to the bag.

Step 4: Sewing the Cosmetic Bag

- Place the fabric pieces' right sides together, aligning the edges, and pin or clip them in place.

- Use a sewing machine to sew along the sides and bottom of the bag, leaving the top open. Backstitch at the beginning and end for added durability.

- Trim any excess fabric and clip the corners to reduce bulk.

- Press the bag's right side out with an iron to create crisp edges.

Step 5: Attaching the Zipper

- Place the zipper face down along the top edge of the bag's opening, aligning the teeth with the fabric edge.

- Use pins or fabric clips to secure the zipper in place.

- Using a zipper foot on your sewing machine, stitch along both sides of the zipper, ensuring you sew close to the teeth.

- Trim any excess zipper length.

Step 6: Finishing Touches

- Turn the bag inside out and topstitch along the top edge, securing the fabric and zipper in place.

- Optional: Add additional embellishments, such as fabric appliques, embroidery, or personalized tags, to enhance the cosmetic bag's aesthetics.

Congratulations! You have successfully created a custom cosmetic bag using Cricut Design Space and the Cricut Maker 3.

Geometric Buffalo Pillows:

Geometric buffalo pillows have become a popular home decor item, adding a touch of rustic charm and modern flair to any space.

Let's dive into the step-by-step guide on how to make a geometric buffalo pillow using Cricut Design Space and the Cricut Maker 3.

Materials Needed:

- Plain fabric pillow cover

- Buffalo design template (available in Cricut Design Space or create your own)

- Cricut Maker 3

- Standard grip mat

- Fabric or iron-on vinyl in desired colors

- Weeding tools

- Iron or heat press

- Iron-on protective sheet (if using iron-on vinyl)

- Pillow insert

Step 1: Designing in Cricut Design Space

- Open Cricut Design Space on your computer or mobile device and create a new project.

- Browse the design library or upload your own geometric buffalo design. Adjust the size and position as desired to fit your pillow cover.

- If using iron-on vinyl, remember to mirror the design horizontally before cutting.

- Proceed to the "**Make**" screen and ensure that the cut settings are appropriate for the selected vinyl type (fabric or iron-on).

Step 2: Cutting the Design

- Connect your Cricut Maker 3 to your computer or mobile device, load the appropriate blade (fine point blade for fabric, or rotary blade for fabric or iron-on vinyl), and place the vinyl on the standard grip mat.

- Follow the on-screen prompts in Cricut Design Space to ensure proper mat loading and calibration.

- Press the "**Start**" button in Design Space to begin cutting the design. The Cricut Maker 3 will precisely cut out the buffalo design from the vinyl.

- Once the cutting is complete, unload the mat from the machine and carefully remove the cut vinyl, using weeding tools if necessary.

Step 3: Applying the Design

- If using fabric vinyl, position the cut vinyl pieces on the fabric pillow cover according to the design. Ensure proper alignment and spacing.

- If using iron-on vinyl, preheat your iron or heat press to the recommended temperature for the specific vinyl type. Place the vinyl on the pillow cover with the carrier sheet facing up. Apply heat and pressure according to the manufacturer's instructions, using an iron-on protective sheet if necessary.

- Allow the vinyl to cool completely before removing the carrier sheet or protective sheet.

Step 4: Finishing Touches

- Once the design is applied and cooled, insert a pillow form or stuffing into the fabric pillow cover.

- Ensure the pillow is evenly distributed and the cover is securely closed.

Congratulations! You have successfully created a stylish geometric buffalo pillow using Cricut Design Space and the Cricut Maker 3.

Customized T-Shirt:

T-shirts with personalized designs continue to be in high demand, whether as a fashion statement, a way to express oneself, or as thoughtful gifts.

With the versatility of Cricut Design Space and the precision of the Cricut Maker 3, you can create your own custom Love inscription T-shirt that is unique and meaningful.

Materials Needed:

- Plain T-shirt of your choice (prewashed and ironed)
- Cricut Maker 3
- Standard grip mat

- Heat transfer vinyl (in desired colors)

- Cricut EasyPress or heat press machine

- Weeding tools

- Scissors or rotary cutter

- Cricut Design Space (installed on your computer or mobile device)

Step 1: Designing in Cricut Design Space

- Open Cricut Design Space on your computer or mobile device and create a new project.

- Browse the design library or create your own Love inscription design using text tools and various design elements. Adjust the size, font, and position as desired.

- Once satisfied with the design, proceed to the "Make" screen and select "Mirror" for each design element to ensure proper application on the T-shirt.

- Connect your Cricut Maker 3 to your computer or mobile device, and load the appropriate heat transfer vinyl color onto the standard grip mat.

Step 2: Cutting the Design

- Follow the on-screen prompts in Cricut Design Space to ensure proper mat loading and calibration.

- Press the "**Start**" button in Design Space to begin cutting the design. The Cricut Maker 3 will precisely cut out the Love inscription design from the heat transfer vinyl.

- Once the cutting is complete, unload the mat from the machine and carefully remove the excess vinyl from around the design using weeding tools.

Step 3: Applying the Design to the T-shirt

- Preheat your Cricut EasyPress or heat press machine to the recommended temperature for the specific heat transfer vinyl and fabric type.

- Place the T-shirt on a heat-resistant surface and position the cut heat transfer vinyl design on the desired location.

- Apply firm and even pressure with the Cricut Easy-Press or heat press machine, following the recommended time and temperature guidelines for the vinyl and fabric.

- Allow the vinyl to cool for a few seconds, then gently peel off the carrier sheet, revealing the Love inscription on the T-shirt.

Step 4: Finishing Touches

- Inspect the applied design to ensure it has adhered properly to the fabric. If any areas require additional heat, use the Cricut EasyPress or heat press machine to apply more pressure as needed.

- Trim any excess vinyl or unwanted parts of the design using scissors or a rotary cutter, ensuring clean edges and a polished look.

Congratulations! You have successfully created your own Love inscription T-shirt using Cricut Design Space and the Cricut Maker 3.

Customized Mugs:

Customized mugs have gained immense popularity as heartfelt and personalized gifts. Whether for special occasions like birthdays or anniversaries or as a token of appreciation, personalized mugs with love inscriptions add a touch of sentiment and thoughtfulness.

Materials Needed:

- Ceramic or porcelain mugs

- Cricut Maker 3

- Cricut Design Space (installed on your computer or mobile device)

- Permanent adhesive vinyl in desired colors

- Cricut Transfer Tape

- Cricut weeding tools

- Cricut EasyPress or household iron

- Heat-resistant tape (if using EasyPress)

- Scissors or craft knife

Step 1: Designing in Cricut Design Space

- Launch Cricut Design Space on your computer or mobile device and create a new project.

- Select or create the design for your love inscription. You can browse the design library or create your own using text tools, shapes, or uploaded images.

- Adjust the size, font, and text alignment to fit your mug. Consider the available space and legibility of the inscription.

- Once satisfied with the design, proceed to the **"Make"**

screen. Ensure that the cut settings are set to "Vinyl" or "Custom" with appropriate settings for the vinyl type.

Step 2: Cutting the Vinyl Design

- Connect your Cricut Maker 3 to your computer or mobile device and load the fine point blade.

- Place the adhesive vinyl onto the standard grip mat, ensuring it is smooth and free from wrinkles or bubbles.

- Follow the on-screen prompts in Cricut Design Space to ensure proper mat loading and calibration.

- Press the "**Start**" button in Design Space to begin cutting the design. The Cricut Maker 3 will precisely cut out the love inscription from the vinyl.

- Once the cutting is complete, unload the mat from the machine and carefully remove the excess vinyl around the design using the weeding tools.

Step 3: Applying the Vinyl Design to the Mug

- Clean the surface of the mug thoroughly with soap and

water, ensuring it is free from any dust, oil, or residue.

- Carefully position the vinyl design onto the mug, ensuring it is straight and centered.

- Use Cricut Transfer Tape to transfer the vinyl design onto the mug. Apply the transfer tape over the design, pressing firmly to adhere it to the vinyl.

- Gently peel off the backing paper, leaving the vinyl design attached to the transfer tape.

- Carefully place the design onto the mug, aligning it with the desired position.

- Press the vinyl onto the mug, starting from the center and working outward, using your fingers or a scraper tool to smooth out any air bubbles or wrinkles.

Step 4: Curing the Vinyl (Optional)

- If using permanent adhesive vinyl, it is recommended to cure the vinyl to ensure long-lasting adherence. Use a Cricut EasyPress or a household iron set to the appropriate temperature for the vinyl and mug material.

- Place a piece of heat-resistant tape over the vinyl design to hold it in place during the heat application process.

- Apply heat and pressure to the vinyl design according to the recommended guidelines for your vinyl and mug material. Follow Cricut's instructions or the vinyl manufacturer's recommendations for the proper time and temperature.

- Allow the mug to cool completely before removing the heat-resistant tape and using or gifting the customized mug.

Congratulations! You have successfully created a personalized mug with a love inscription using Cricut Design Space and the Cricut Maker 3.

Remember to hand wash the mugs gently to ensure the longevity of the vinyl design. Enjoy sipping beverages from your customized mugs or delight someone special with a thoughtful and personalized gift.

Customized Mug:

The demand for personalized and customized cards has skyrocketed. Whether for birthdays, weddings, holidays, or special occasions, people seek unique and heartfelt ways to express their emotions through custom-made cards.

With the Cricut Design Space and Cricut Maker 3, you have the power to create stunning customized cards that will leave a lasting impression.

Materials Needed:

- Cardstock or specialty paper in desired colors

- Cricut Maker 3

- Standard grip mat

- Fine Point Blade or appropriate blade for your chosen material

- Cricut Design Space (installed on your computer or mobile device)

- Adhesive or glue

- Embellishments (such as ribbons, stickers, or gems)

- Scissors or paper trimmer

Step 1: Designing in Cricut Design Space

- Launch Cricut Design Space on your computer or mobile device and create a new project.

- Select the card template or create a custom card design by combining various shapes, images, and text elements. Customize the size, orientation, and colors to suit your preferences.

- Ensure that the cut settings are set to "**Cardstock**" or the appropriate setting for the type of paper you are using.

- Connect your Cricut Maker 3 to your computer or mobile device, load the fine point blade, and place the cardstock on the standard grip mat.

Step 2: Cutting the Card Design

- Follow the on-screen prompts in Cricut Design Space to ensure proper mat loading and calibration.

- Press the "**Start**" button in Design Space to initiate the cutting process. The Cricut Maker 3 will accurately cut out the card design from the cardstock, including any intricate details or decorative elements.

- Once the cutting is complete, unload the mat from the machine and carefully remove the cut cardstock pieces from the mat.

Step 3: Assembling the Card

- Fold the cardstock along the designated score lines to create the desired card shape.

- Apply adhesive or glue to the designated areas on the cardstock, ensuring even coverage.

- Carefully align and press the cardstock pieces together to assemble the card, following the design from Cricut Design Space.

- Allow the adhesive to dry according to the manufacturer's instructions.

Step 4: Personalization and Embellishments

- Add a personal touch to your customized card by including a heartfelt message or personalized sentiment using a pen or marker.

- Enhance the card's visual appeal by adding embellishments like ribbons, stickers, gems, or any other decorative elements that complement the design and occasion.

- Trim any excess paper or tidy up any edges using scissors or a paper trimmer for a polished finish.

Step 5: Final Touches

- Carefully inspect the card for any remaining adhesive residue or imperfections, and remove them if necessary.

- Open the card and ensure it folds and closes smoothly.

- Give your customized card a final check for any necessary adjustments or additions before presenting or sending it to your intended recipient.

Congratulations! You have successfully created a stunning customized card using Cricut Design Space and the Cricut Maker 3.

Halloween Mask:

Halloween masks are essential to the festive season, allowing people to transform into their favorite characters, creatures, or spooky beings.

With the growing popularity of Halloween celebrations, there is an increasing demand for unique and personalized masks.

Materials Needed:

- Cricut Maker 3

- Standard grip mat

- Fine Point Blade

- Cardstock or specialty paper in desired colors

- Elastic cord or ribbon for mask attachment

- Scissors

- Glue or adhesive tape

- Cricut Design Space (installed on your computer or mobile device)

Step 1: Designing the Halloween Mask in Cricut Design Space

- Open Cricut Design Space on your computer or mobile device and create a new project.

- Browse through the Design Space library for Halloween mask designs, or upload your own mask design if desired.

- Adjust the size, orientation, and position of the mask design to fit your preferences.

- Once satisfied with the design, proceed to the "**Make**" screen and ensure that the cut settings are set to "Cardstock" or the appropriate material you're using.

- Connect your Cricut Maker 3 to your computer or mobile device, load the fine point blade, and place the cardstock or specialty paper on the standard grip mat.

Step 2: Cutting the Halloween Mask Design

- Follow the on-screen prompts in Cricut Design Space to ensure proper mat loading and calibration.

- Press the "**Start**" button in Design Space to begin cutting the mask design. The Cricut Maker 3 will accurately cut out the intricate details of the mask from the cardstock or specialty paper.

- Once the cutting is complete, carefully unload the mat from the machine and remove the cut mask pieces from the mat.

Step 3: Assembling and Finishing the Halloween Mask

- Use scissors to carefully cut out any remaining inner sections of the mask, such as eye holes or mouth openings.

- Apply glue or adhesive tape to the designated tabs on

the mask pieces, following the assembly instructions provided in Design Space.

- Carefully fold and adhere to the tabs to create the three-dimensional shape of the mask.

- Attach the elastic cord or ribbon to the sides of the mask to secure it to your face. Measure and cut the elastic cord or ribbon to the desired length, then secure each end to the mask using glue or by creating small slits and tying knots.

Step 4: Personalization and Embellishments

- Let your creativity shine by personalizing the Halloween mask. You can add additional decorative elements, such as feathers, sequins, or paint, to enhance the overall look.

- Customize the mask with colors, patterns, or themed embellishments that align with your desired Halloween character or theme.

Fifty (50) Project Idea:

Here are 50 Cricut project ideas to get you started:

1. Custom t-shirts

2. Personalized mugs

3. Custom invitations

4. Wall decals

5. Paper flowers

6. Stenciled pillows

7. Custom phone cases

8. Fabric bags

9. Paper garlands

10. Embroidered patches

11. Scrapbook layouts

12. Personalized notebooks

13. Custom coasters

14. Wall art

15. Paper lanterns

16. Stenciled tote bags

17. Paper earrings

18. Custom gift tags

19. Monogrammed towels

20. Scrapbook paper wreaths

21. Fabric headbands

22. Custom magnets

23. Paper lantern garlands

24. Embroidered hats

25. Stenciled placemats

26. Fabric bows

27. Custom jewelry

28. Scrapbook paper garlands

29. Personalized pens

30. Custom keychains

31. Wall decals for kids' rooms

32. Paper lantern mobile

33. Embroidered patches for jean jackets

34. Custom postcards

35. Scrapbook paper flowers

36. Fabric bows for hair

37. Monogrammed wine glasses

38. Custom gift wrap

39. Wall art for the kitchen

40. Paper lantern party decorations

41. Stenciled pillowcases

42. Fabric headbands for kids

43. Custom stickers

44. Scrapbook paper garlands for parties

45. Personalized pencil cases

46. Custom bookmarks

47. Wall decals for the bathroom

48. Paper lanterns for weddings

49. Embroidered

50. Halloween Mask

RATE THIS BOOK

Dear Valued Reader,

Warm greetings to you! I hope this message finds you thriving and full of literary enthusiasm. As a self-publishing author, I write to you today with a humble request for a review of this book.

Behind every book lies a tale of devotion—a testament to the countless hours poured into its creation. My dedicated team and I have spared no effort in meticulously gathering and curating the wealth of information encapsulated within these pages.

Dear valued reader, we aim to provide you with a valuable collection of insightful information, thorough research, and practical knowledge regarding your Cricut Machine. We invested both money and time into creating this book.

Therefore, your feedback holds immeasurable value in our journey. Please take a few moments to leave a review on Amazon. Click on this **Link** or visit (*www.amazon.com/review/create-review?&asin=B0CCMSTXLQ*) to rate this book.

Your comments will tell us how well we perform and guide fellow readers from the extensive wisdom we have painstakingly compiled. We are eagerly awaiting to hear your thoughts and insights. Thank you for considering our request. We appreciate your review and comments, and we will keep them in mind.